THE DECLINE OF
INLAND BILLS OF EXCHANGE IN
THE LONDON MONEY MARKET
1855–1913

THE DECLINE OF INLAND BILLS OF EXCHANGE IN THE LONDON MONEY MARKET 1855–1913

SHIZUYA NISHIMURA

Assistant Professor, Faculty of Business Administration, Hosei University, Tokyo

CAMBRIDGE
AT THE UNIVERSITY PRESS
1971

Published by the Syndics of the Cambridge University Press
Bentley House, 200 Euston Road, London NW1 2DB
American Branch: 32 East 57th Street, New York, N.Y.10022

© Cambridge University Press 1971

Library of Congress Catalogue Card Number: 70–134613

ISBN: 0 521 08055 X

Printed in Great Britain
at the University Printing House, Cambridge
(Brooke Crutchley, University Printer)

CONTENTS

TABLES

FIGURES

PREFACE

My interest in British monetary history was first aroused when I was a graduate student at the University of Tokyo. It was in the middle years of the fifties, when the memory of our defeat in the Pacific War was still fresh and, although the reconstruction of the economy had by that time been completed and the first spurt of its vigorous development was already in evidence, Japan was still worlds behind the nations of Western Europe and North America. It was thought that the process of industrialization of these mature economies would provide us with lessons for our future development. This feeling led many, perhaps too many, students to the study of the economic histories of the advanced countries in Europe and America, and I was one of them. I took up the study of the amalgamation movement in English banking. The intention was to compare the process of bank concentration in Japan with that in England. Fortunately I was awarded a British Council scholarship for the academic year 1960–1, and I could travel around England in quest of materials for my research. Thus I was able to visit a number of public libraries as well as the British Museum. It was in the course of this research that I came to sense something odd about the commonly-accepted explanation of the decline of inland bills. Needless to say, it was Dr W. T. C. King who ascribed the phenomenon to the amalgamation movement among banks. However, the movement really accelerated only in the nineties of the nineteenth century, while inland bills had already begun to decrease from about 1873. On the other hand, from the verbal evidence of contemporaries I obtained the impression that the revolution in transport and communication after the seventies had a great deal to do with the process.

A year was, however, too short a space of time to make a deeper investigation of the topic. After I returned to Japan, I negotiated with Hosei University, with which I had obtained a teaching post, to give me a special leave of absence to resume the study in England, and I am in deep debt to the University as well as to my colleagues in its Faculty of Business Administration for permitting me to go to England every other year.

Thus I was able to take up the study again at the London School of Economics under the supervision of Dr L. S. Pressnell, to whom I am immensely indebted in a number of ways. Although I had constructed my own hypothesis of the causes of the decline of internal bills, there were some gaps in my logic, of which I had not been aware and which he was quick enough to point out. I must also say that he was such a demanding teacher that he thrust upon me seemingly impossible tasks.

I have somehow complied with his exacting demands and the result is this book. I am particularly grateful to him for his advice to treat the topic statistically, for before I met him I limited myself almost entirely to finding suitable verbal evidence. Also he corrected my faulty English at a number of places in the text. But, of course, the faults in this book are entirely my own.

I received a grant in aid of research in connection with a section of this book from the Central Research Fund of the University of London. A slightly different version of this study has been accepted by the University of London as a thesis for the degree of Ph.D. in economics.

My thanks are due to Kinyu Keizai Kenkyu Sho (The Institute for Banking and Financial Research Inc.), a subsidiary organization of the Mitsui Bank, which published the Japanese version of my thesis in its bi-monthly, *Kinyu Keizai* (*The Journal of Financial Economics*), and also kindly permitted without reservation the publication of my thesis in book form.

I am indebted to Professor Kohachiro Takahashi, Professor Toshihiko Kato and Professor Takao Takeda of the University of Tokyo, as well as to Professor Sahei Watanabe of Hosei University, for initiating me into the study of British monetary history. Professor R. S. Sayers gave me some valuable suggestions at the time of my oral examination, which I have incorporated in this book. Miss S. Baseden of the London School of Economics has kindly typed the draft for me. In conclusion, I wish to pay tribute to my late father and to my wife. My father, who was teaching English literature at a university, delayed his retirement to finance a part of my study in England. I am infinitely grateful to my wife for her encouragement, help and forbearance. While I was studying in England, she had to stay behind in Japan. She also made a double check of the statistical figures in the thesis.

S. N.

April 1970

NOTES

1   Years are financial years, unless otherwise mentioned; i.e. 1855 means the year commencing April 1855 and ending March 1856.
2   BPP stands for British Parliamentary Papers.

INTRODUCTION

It is a well established generalization that the supply of inland bills of exchange in the London discount market experienced a sharp fall after the seventies of the nineteenth century and that thereafter the main business of the market became the discount of foreign bills. It is said from this that the chief function of the market changed from the finance of domestic trade to that of international trade. Both of these propositions need qualification, as will appear later.

W. T. C. King, in his *History of the London Discount Market*, tried to explain the causes of the decline of domestic bills in the following words. He wrote,

By far the most important of these new influences was the bank amalgamation movement, bringing with it a great expansion of branch banking, and enabling many banks to perform within its own organization the 'equalizing' function for which the bill market had previously been indispensable....After 1878...the era of really large-scale banking began. In consequence, the number of branch banks, which had risen by some 35 per cent. to 2,413 in the nine years to 1881, increased by a further 40 per cent. to 3,383 in the ensuing decade. This development, by enabling the bigger banks to finance from the deposits of their 'agricultural' branches the demands at their 'industrial' branches, removed one of the principal reasons for the use of the bills as the standard instrument of accommodation. From many points of view, it became a matter of indifference to the banks whether they financed their customers by discounting their bills or by granting loans or advances, and to the customers the flexibility of the overdraft system had definite attractions. Thus the spread of branch banks was accompanied in many trades by a gradual displacement of the internal bill by the 'open credit' system as the standard means of finance.[1]

[1] W. T. C. King, *History of the London Discount Market*, London, 1936, p. 273.
    It must be conceded that King refers to other causes of the decline of internal bills. He writes (p. 274), 'Meanwhile, other influences were working in the same direction. The improvement in communications, accelerating the speed with which goods moved to market and into final consumption, was shortening the customary credit terms; the growth of the industrial combine, making it increasingly difficult for the head office of a business to watch the many bills of its retailer customers, and to ensure due payment at maturity, was producing a marked preference for cash payments, or at least for credit by ledger accounts; and a new and vigorous business competition was popularizing a system of cash rebates which made payment by bills definitely unprofitable. At the same time, the growth of the banking habit, and the availability of banking facilities in every important town, put an end to the use of bills as local currency.' As will appear later, there are some points here, in which I concur in explaining the decline of inland bills, but on the whole such impressionistic expositions are hardly sufficient for precise analysis. Moreover, there are obvious difficulties with some of these explanations. Industrial combines would experience the same difficulty and trouble in ensuring due payment at maturity either of bills or of ledger accounts of their retailer customers. On the other hand, bills are more convenient for industrial combines, because they can discount the bills when need be, whereas ledger accounts are not a liquid form of assets. If there were such developments, therefore, the reason must be sought, not in the numerousness of the retailer customers, but in the circumstance that industrial combines had more ample resources so that they had no need to discount the bills in their hands and it was immaterial for them whether they held their assets in the form of bills or ledger accounts. Secondly, rebate on cash payments has

R. G. Hawtrey, in his *A Century of Bank Rate*, endorsed the above opinion of King in almost identical words,[1] and thereafter King's argument has come to be almost unanimously accepted by monetary historians. As recently as 1968, W. M. Scammell writes as follows,

The main reason for this decline [of inland bills] lay in the changes taking place at that time in the structure of the banking system. The old unitary banking system of the first part of the nineteenth century was giving way to a concentrated banking system working through a branch network. This made easy the transference of liquid funds from district to district and enabled the old 'equalising function', performed by the country banks and their practice of rediscounting, to be superseded. The overdraft and bank loan became common as means of financing short-term trade credit and their use grew as a result of their flexibility and convenience.[2]

The above hypothesis of King and others is by no means a result of a detailed study of the phenomenon, but is of the nature of a sketchy impression. There are certain difficulties with the argument. For one thing, the appearance of large-scale banks with balanced nation-wide branch networks is a comparatively recent phenomenon. They are largely products of the amalgamation movement among banks and this movement accelerated particularly in the nineties. Before the nineties there was only one such bank in England and Wales, namely the National Provincial Bank of England. If we take for instance the year 1885, we find only eight banks with more than 50 offices (i.e. including head offices, branches, sub-branches, agencies and sub-agencies, but excluding London agencies of country banks). They are London and County Banking Co. (162 offices), National Provincial Bank of England (155 offices), Capital and Counties Bank (98 offices), London and Provincial Bank (88 offices), Wilts and Dorset Banking Co. (78 offices), Manchester and Liverpool District Banking Co. (69 offices), North and South Wales Bank (66 offices), and London and South-Western Bank (54 offices). Of these, London and County, Capital and Counties, London and South-Western, and London and Provincial had head offices in London and their branches were mainly scattered in the London suburbs and the southern counties of England (which were, of course, largely agricultural or residential districts). Wilts and Dorset, North and South Wales, and Manchester and Liverpool District were

traditionally been given at attractive rates probably since the eighteenth century, although the rate seems to have fluctuated with the business cycle. (See L. S. Pressnell, 'The Rate of Interest in the Eighteenth Century' in *Studies in the Industrial Revolution* (ed. by Pressnell), London, 1960, pp. 199–200.) If cash payments became the order of the day, therefore, there must have been forces at work which enabled firms to pay in cash more than formerly.

[1] R. G. Hawtrey, *A Century of Bank Rate*, 2nd ed., London, 1962, p. 55.

[2] W. M. Scammell, *The London Discount Market*, London, 1968, p. 29. Faithfully reflecting King, Scammell points to other causes of the decline of inland bills. 'Apart from this, changes in the structure of business itself—a shortening of periods of trade credit, a preference by firms for cash settlement and a growing measure of competition—made the bill of exchange less attractive as a medium of payment than formerly.' (*Ibid.*, p. 29.)

local banks (North and South Wales Bank may be said to have possessed a balanced branch network, for its head office was in Liverpool and the branches were located mainly in North Wales). Thus, with the exception of the National Provincial Bank, there were at this time no banks capable of performing such functions as the transference of liquid funds from 'agricultural' areas to industrial counties.

On the other hand, the estimated amount of bills drawn began to decline from the financial year 1873, when it was £1,781 m. The decrease continued till the financial year 1894, when it was £1,121 m. (Years hereafter are financial years and 1873 means the year commencing April 1873 and ending March 1874.) If we take the amount of inland bills drawn, it was £721 m. in 1870 and was £490 m. in 1894. (The method of estimation of the volume of bills drawn will be discussed in Chapter 2.)

Moreover, the volume of inland bills coming to the London discount market must have experienced a much more drastic reduction than the figures of the amounts of bills drawn would seem to suggest. For the latter quantity will depend upon the following three factors: (1) the amount of bills drawn, (2) the average usance of bills, (3) the proportion of bills retained till maturity by the drawers themselves or by the local banks which had discounted the bills. We have evidence that the values of both (2) and (3) underwent considerable changes during the period in question. It is not inconceivable even that the supply of internal bills in the London discount market was diminishing before 1873, although the amount of inland bills drawn in each year was strongly on the increase during the period 1855–73. On this point there is evidence by William Fowler, a noted banker, who stated that rediscounting of bills by country banks 'rapidly reduced after 1857'.[1]

There is thus a gap of at least twenty years between the decline of the amount of inland bills in the London money market and the emergence of mammoth banks with branch offices all over the country. It is difficult to see how one can explain a phenomenon of the seventies by an occurrence of the nineties.

In the following pages I wish to criticize King's hypothesis. I wish to do that mainly by attaching statistical values to the argument and I hope in the process to be able to produce an alternative explanation of the decline of inland bills.

Chapter 1 deals with the development of branch banking. Chapters 2, 3 and 4 aim at estimating the supply of bills, both inland and foreign, in the London discount market. As has been shown, the supply of bills in Lombard Street depends upon (1) the amount of bills drawn, (2) the average usance of bills and (3) the proportion of bills retained till

[1] 'Inaugural Address by William Fowler', *Journal of the Institute of Bankers*, 1891, p. 618.

maturity by the drawers and the local banks. The relationship may be expressed in a simple algebraic form as follows:

$$S_{\mathrm{BL}} = \frac{U}{12}\left(1 - \left(\frac{B_{\mathrm{rd}}}{B_{\mathrm{D}}} + \frac{B_{\mathrm{rb}}}{B_{\mathrm{D}}}\right)\right) B_{\mathrm{D}},$$

where S_{BL} stands for the supply of bills in the London discount market, U for the number of months of the average usance of bills, B_{D} for the amount of bills drawn, B_{rd} for the volume of bills retained till maturity by drawers and B_{rb} for the quantity of bills retained by local banks.

Chapters 2, 3 and 4 deal respectively with each member of the right-hand side of the above equation; i.e. Chapter 2 is devoted to the estimation of the amount of bills drawn in each financial year during the period 1855–1913, and Chapter 3 deals with the change in the average usance of bills during the period, while Chapter 4 aims at estimating the amount of bills discounted by banks. I must stress that the results obtained in these chapters are more or less in the nature of tentative approximations and that they may be liable to great margins of error. The estimated amounts of bills are, however, more reliable, since the estimation is based upon the more or less solid ground of the statistics of revenues from the sale of stamps for bills of exchange. The average usance of bills is estimated from the balance-sheets of two banks, Parr's Bank and Liverpool Union Bank, which state the amount of bills discounted, rebate of discount on bills in hand and the rate of discount applied to the calculation of the rebate. Besides this, considerable evidence on this point was given before the royal commissions and the select committees of the period. In addition, *The Economist*, *The Statist* and *Bankers' Magazine* are helpful in this respect. The volume of bills retained till maturity by the drawers themselves cannot be known. Bills retained by local banks, too, cannot be known precisely, especially before 1870, for published balance-sheets of banks are notoriously defective. For example, in 1867 only eleven banks clearly showed the amounts of bills discounted. Even in 1880 only thirty-one banks showed the breakdown between advances and discounts. The results obtained, therefore, purport to show only broad tendencies.

Chapter 5 deals with the tendency to cash payment, which King points out and which contemporaries thought to be the chief cause of the decline of the use of bills.

Chapter 6 deals with the change in the general character of bills which was caused by the decrease of inland bills and the increase of foreign bills, and also with some consequences of the change. A word of caution is in order here. It is customary to say that at the same time as internal bills decreased foreign bills increased to take their place, and that the chief function of the London discount market became the finance of international trade. But the fact is that foreign bills decreased hand in hand with domestic bills (although to a smaller extent than inland bills) during the years 1873–94, and so there developed a shortage of both inland bills and foreign bills in the market. The great increase in the amount of foreign bills took place only after 1894.

A further qualification is necessary to the above dictum. The distinction between inland bills and foreign bills is largely a legal one and does not necessarily show the difference in the nature of transactions behind the two kinds of bills. It would be rather naive to suppose that the London discount market was financing purely domestic trade before the seventies when domestic bills were predominant in the market, whereas after that the market came to finance international trade because foreign bills came to dominate. Inland bills were very often drawn to finance the export trade of the United Kingdom and therefore in a sense a part (or rather a greater portion) of inland bills on London were instruments for financing the foreign trade of the country. On the other hand, not all the foreign bills were drawn for the finance of international trade. Some of them were finance bills drawn in order to effect the international movement of short-term capital.

1. BANK OFFICES IN ENGLAND AND WALES, 1855–1913

As we have already seen, King puts great emphasis on the increase in the number of bank offices and the development of branch banking in explaining the causes of the decline in the use of inland bills. But he does not give any precise statistics to prove his points save very rough figures of the total number of bank branches: namely, he points out that the number of branch banks increased by 35% to 2,413 in the nine years to 1881, and that in the ensuing decade the number increased by a further 40% to 3,383. These figures relate to England and Wales and are quoted by King from Sykes, *The Amalgamation Movement in English Banking*,[1] and Sykes, in turn, quotes these figures from *Banking Almanac*.

There can be two criticisms of King's argument on this point. First, since he puts great stress on the transference of funds from agricultural areas to industrial counties, which is done in the framework of one and the same bank, it is not enough merely to enumerate the total number of bank branches. The relevant statistics would have been the number of branches per bank.

The second criticism is that the number of bank offices in England and Wales was increasing at a fairly regular pace from the middle of the nineteenth century and that the seventies and the eighties were not the only decades during which their numbers increased significantly.

According to my own calculation the number of bank offices (which includes head offices) in England and Wales was 1,225 in 1861, and increased to 1,647 in 1871, or by 34%. It was 2,256 in 1881, an increase of 37% compared with 1871. In 1891 it was 3,213, an increase of just about 42% over 1881. During the ten years 1891–1901 it increased by 47% to 4,726. From 1901 to 1911 it grew by 30% to 6,127.

It is difficult to believe that only the 35% increase in the seventies and the 40% increase in the eighties (percentage figures according to King) were material in reducing the volume of inland bills, and that the 34% increase during the sixties and the 47% increase during the nineties did not have an equally decisive influence in this matter.

I have made my own investigation of the number of bank offices in England and Wales for the period 1855–1913. As the issue at stake is the progress of branch banking, the number of bank offices in Scotland and Ireland is not investigated, because in those countries branch

---

[1] J. Sykes, *The Amalgamation Movement in English Banking, 1825–1924*, London, 1926, p. 113. His figures as well as those of *Banking Almanac* are inappropriate. See Appendix to Table 1.

banking was already highly developed by the middle of the nineteenth century.

The main material used was, of course, *Banking Almanac* (*Bankers' Almanac* after 1920). Each issue of *Banking Almanac* generally records the number of bank offices in October of the year immediately preceding. But we should be careful in using the *Almanac*, for it is by no means an absolutely reliable source for the following reasons:

(1) It does not distinguish between genuine home banks and other financial institutions, e.g. merchant bankers, bill-brokers, credit agents, foreign bankers and so on. This defect becomes most troublesome when we deal with banks in great financial centres, such as London, Liverpool and Manchester, where there is scope for specialization in financial activities.

Needless to say, there cannot be any hard and fast rule by which to judge what is a genuine home bank and what is not such a bank. This is possibly a matter to be decided by common sense. Of course, there was a legal way of defining a bank. Legally a bank could be defined as a firm which was entitled to claim payment in cash over the counter of a crossed cheque which it held on its own account or on its customers' account. To be able to do this a bank had to be registered with the Inland Revenue Office. But this registration unfortunately is not a very good guide in identifying a home bank. For one thing joint stock companies were exempt from this duty of registration in conducting banking. In most such cases, the titles of the companies provide a clue. Then, those banks duly registered include a large body of merchant bankers and foreign banks and others (e.g. Gillett Bros., bill-brokers, and Samuel, Montagu, merchant bankers, are both included among the registered banks).[1]

It may be thought that membership of the Bankers' Clearing House would be a good guide in this respect. But many banks which must have passed as genuine home banks were non-clearing banks in this period. Traditionally a group of private banks in the City controlled the London clearing, and joint-stock banks experienced considerable difficulty in obtaining membership. For example, London and Provincial Bank, which had 344 offices in 1913 and was the seventh largest bank in England and Wales, was not a member.[2]

Therefore, one has to rely to a great extent on the contemporary

---

[1] 7 and 8 Vict., cap. 32 (Section 21) stipulates the registration of banks. 45 and 46 Vict., cap. 72 (Section 11) exempts joint stock companies conducting banking from this duty. By the way, London clearing banks have decided not to avail themselves of this privilege of claiming the payment over the counter of crossed cheques and instead exchange the cheques at the clearing.

[2] At first, joint-stock banks were denied the right to join the Clearing House. It was only in June 1854 that some of them, including London and Westminster Bank, obtained membership. (See T. E. Gregory, *The Westminster Bank through a Century*, London, 1936, pp. 173–4.)

common-sense labelling in determining what is to be regarded as a genuine home bank. In the case of London this information is fortunately supplied by such publications as *Post Office London Directory*, *Handbook of London Banks and Bankers*, by Hilton Price, and *London Banks and Kindred Companies and Firms*, edited by Thomas Skinner. Of these the last-mentioned is of the most use, for it endeavours to show the nature of each firm's business.[1]

But these directories relate only to London. In the case of Liverpool and Manchester there is no such source of information. Only in one instance have I been able to weed out a merchant banker from the list, i.e. E. L. Samuel & Co., which moved to London in 1869 to join in the firm of Samuel, Montagu & Co.

(2) The earlier issues of the Almanac fail to record many banks, which begin to appear in it for the first time long after their formation. Sometimes the Almanac does give the years of their foundation, but in these cases, too, doubt arises as to the exact numbers of offices of such banks during the years in which they do not appear in the Almanac. In such cases I gave the value of unity to these banks in regard to their number of offices during those unclear years. And in very many instances the Almanac does not show the years of formation of these banks.

(3) In the case of country private banks *Banking Almanac* very often records the same bank over and over again as existing at the several places where the offices of the bank exist; e.g. Cunliffes, Brooks & Co. is represented three times as existing in Blackburn, Manchester and Altrincham. Then, there are cases of apparently different banks with slightly different partnerships, but in actual fact belonging to the same entity. For instance, the Gurneys of Norwich are related to Gurneys of Great Yarmouth, Fakenham, King's Lynn, Ipswich and Wisbech. There are many instances of such loose federation and it is very often difficult to determine whether they should be treated as one bank or as separate units. This again is largely a matter for discretion. I treated these federated banks as separate units unless it is clearly stated in the Almanac that a bank is a subsidiary of another bank. In the above example of the Gurneys, the Fakenham bank is indicated as a branch of the Gurneys of Norwich, but the other banks do not carry such identification.

(4) In the case of joint-stock banks there are those occupying the intermediate sphere between genuine home banking and other fields of

---

[1] The publication of this directory started in 1865 under the name of *The London Banks, Credit, Discount and Finance Companies*; it was incorporated in *Bankers' Almanac* in 1919. After 1880 it began to accord to each firm the designation of its business. It says, 'It is incidental to such an effort that it should not meet with entire approbation, but the object in view is so obviously useful, especially to foreign users of the book...' (T. Skinner, *The London Banks and Kindred Companies and Firms*, London, 1880, pp. 3–4.)

financial activity. For example, the Birkbeck Bank was a company which combined deposit banking and the functions of a building society. There are others like Reliance Bank (the savings bank of the Salvation Army), Co-operative Wholesale Society, Harrod's Stores Bank, Farrow's Bank (industrial provident society) and so on. Notably there was one 'bank' called Whiteley & Co. Ltd, which employed most of its resources in freehold estate. All these are listed as 'banks' in *Banking Almanac*. Fortunately, most joint-stock banks published their balance-sheets, so that in most cases we can distinguish genuine home banks from others by looking at them. (Of course, we cannot distinguish between a home bank and a foreign or a colonial bank by balance-sheets, but here the titles of banks give us the clue.)

(5) Most probably there are errors in *Banking Almanac*.

It is, therefore, almost impossible to arrive at absolutely accurate statistics of bank offices in England and Wales, if we rely on *Banking Almanac* alone. For our present purposes, however, statistics based on it may suffice, for it is the only exhaustive survey of banks in this period and the results obtained from it are unlikely to be very far wide of the mark.

The results of my investigation are shown in Table 1. From it we can see that the number of offices per bank was 3·1 in 1861, 4·5 in 1871, 6·7 in 1881, 12·3 in 1891, 30·7 in 1901 and 77·6 in 1911. If we take joint-stock banks only, the figures are: 6·9 in 1861, 9·2 in 1871, 12·9 in 1881, 23·1 in 1891, 56·2 in 1901 and 126·9 in 1911. It is evident from this that the great leap forward in the number of offices per bank commenced from the nineties.

Table 2 gives the names of banks with more than 100 offices and from it we can see that until 1886 there were only two such banks, i.e. National Provincial Bank and London & County Bank. It was in 1889 that Lloyds Bank came to possess more than 100 offices, while the Midland reached that point in 1893. Barclays was formed in 1896 out of fifteen private banks, while the Westminster Bank became a nation-wide bank only after 1909, when it amalgamated with London & County Bank. Thus, it becomes evident from a glance at the table that the formation of big banks with national networks of branches is a feature of the nineties, although the National Provincial Bank had been a national bank ever since its foundation in 1833.

Another point which contradicts King's hypothesis is that banks in Lancashire and Yorkshire kept comparatively aloof from the bank amalgamation movement. Since it was from Lancashire and the West Riding of Yorkshire that the greater part of inland bills were sent to London in the middle of the nineteenth century, the linking of Lancashire and West Riding banks with those in 'agricultural' areas would have been necessary for the use of inland bills as a means of the transference of money to have been effectively discontinued. Nothing of the sort happened save in one case, that of the amalgamation of Parr's Bank, originally of Warrington in Lancashire, with Stuckey's Banking Company of Somersetshire. This fusion is an ideal case for King's hypothesis, but unfortunately this occurred in 1909, much later than the decline in the use of inland bills.

Further, it should be recalled that agriculture was particularly hard hit in the Great Depression of the last quarter of the nineteenth century, when agricultural depopulation was in progress. In the circumstances, we would scarcely expect banks in agricultural areas to be as prosperous as they were in the middle of the century. Former agricultural areas in the South of England were, however, apparently becoming more prosperous, judging from the proliferation of bank offices in these districts after the seventies and from the great increase in deposits of banks situated in these districts. Apparently this is a consequence of the increase in income from abroad and, in the case of London suburbs, of the growth of salaried classes. It might, therefore, be misleading to use the term 'agricultural' in the cases of banks like Stuckeys, London & County, Wilts and Dorset, Capital & Counties and so on. The counties in which these banks were situated may more aptly be termed residential or rentier districts.

In this connection, it must be added that it is not supposed that the increase in the number of bank offices had nothing to do with the decline in the use of inland bills. As banks in industrial cities came to be able to absorb more savings deposits by setting up branches in the suburbs, their position became more liquid. With more liquidity these banks became better able to hold till maturity the discounted bills which they had previously sent to London for re-discount. It would, then, become immaterial to them if they accommodated industry by the discount of bills or by overdraft. If the banks' customers became able to use the facilities of overdraft more liberally than formerly, they would cease to pay by bills (i.e. by permitting their creditors to draw upon them), and use cheques in payment, thereby gaining the rebate on cash payment.

This is substantially the same argument as King's, but the difference is that we need not consider that the linking of 'industrial' banks with 'agricultural' banks is the necessary pre-condition for the decline of inland bills.[1] Quite apart from such a movement, the position of banks in industrial counties was changing radically during the period in question, as will be seen in Chapter 5.

[1] This may be a slight overstatement. According to Sayers, Gillett Bros., bill-brokers, had a small amount of country bills in their portfolio even in 1905 and, as country banks were absorbed one by one by London banks, the flow of bills from the country to the London firm tapered off. See R. S. Sayers, *Gilletts in the London Money Market 1867–1967*, Oxford, 1968, p. 48.

2. ESTIMATED AMOUNTS OF
BILLS DRAWN, 1855–1913

I HISTORY OF THE ESTIMATION OF
THE AMOUNTS OF BILLS DRAWN

It was W. Leatham, a banker of Wakefield, Yorkshire, who first made an effort to ascertain the amounts of bills drawn. The data he used were the statistics of stamp duties on bills of exchange. He writes,

I take, then, for the basis, the return of bill stamps made by the Stamp Office. After discovering the medium sum which each denomination of stamp bears or carries, by an inspection of bills running, I then proceed to ascertain the mean or average rate at which bills are drawn; some at three months, above and below that rate. On a reference to the mass of bills in my own Bill-cases and taking the seven days' experience of the two leading Bill-brokers in the City, I find so near an agreement in all, that I am fully warranted in assuming the average date to be three months.[1]

My next step to ascertain the proportion of foreign bills circulating to the whole of the inland bills had been attended with more difficulty; but in the absence of other concurring testimony, I have to rest on the return kindly furnished by the leading bill-brokers' firm in the City, of the result of seven days' business, and I find it is one-fifth; but in order to err on the safe side, I take it at one-sixth of the whole of the inland bills.[2]

By this method he estimated the amount of inland bills drawn in the United Kingdom, for the calendar years 1815, 1824, 1825; for July 1826 to June 1827; for calendar years 1832, 1833, 1834, 1835, 1836, 1837, 1838 and 1839. The scale of stamp duties for the period 1815–54 is shown in Table 3.

It is evident from Table 3 that the usance of the bill as well as the amount of the bill mattered and that the range in the amount of bills for one kind of stamp was a very wide one. For example, an 8s. 6d. stamp was applied to bills in the range £300–£1,000. Leatham states that the average amount of bills on each class of stamps was determined by his own experience and uses the amount of £875 as the average sum of bills on 8s. 6d. stamps. Such a procedure will make the results of estimation liable to a large margin of error. However, his results are shown in Table 4.

Newmarch was the next person to make the endeavour. He made two series of estimates; the first is the yearly estimates of bills drawn in Great Britain for the years 1828–47,[3] and the second is the quarterly

---

[1] W. Leatham, (First Series) *Letters on the Currency addressed to Charles Wood*, London, 1840, 2nd ed., pp. 54–5. [2] *Ibid.*, p. 55.
[3] W. Newmarch, 'An Attempt to Ascertain the Magnitude and Fluctuation of the Amount of Bills of Exchange (Inland and Foreign) in Circulation at one time in Great Britain...', *Journal of the Statistical Society*, 1851.

estimates of bills drawn in England and Wales for the years 1830–53.[1] Newmarch's method of estimation is a much more refined one than that of Leatham's. He writes,

How, then, can the mere elements of the calculation rendered by the Stamp Office be turned to profitable account? Obviously, only by one method, and that method must consist in ascertaining, from a careful and systematic examination of a large number of real and bona fide bills of exchange drawn upon 3s. 6d. stamps, two facts, namely, (1) the average amount of each bills, and (2) the average usance of each bill.[2]

(3s. 6d. stamps here are just an example quoted to illustrate the mode of estimation.)

Thus, in 1849 he sent questionnaires to five banking houses (four bankers and one bill-broker) to obtain the particulars of 4,367 bills amounting to £1,216,884. The summary result of this survey is reproduced in Table 5. From this he calculated the average amounts of bills on each class of stamps. Then, he used the statistics of revenue from stamps on bills to calculate the total amounts of bills drawn for the period 1828–47.[3] Then, he divided the estimated amount of bills drawn in each year by the reciprocal of the ratio of the average number of months of usance to 12 months. The quotient obtained shows the amount of bills in circulation at one time in each year. From the figures I calculated back the amounts of bills drawn and they are shown in Table 6. (Newmarch as well as Leatham made the calculation to the order of thousands, but it is obvious that in this kind of guesswork, liable to a large margin of error, such fine figures as thousands of pounds are meaningless and so I give the figures only to the order of millions.)

The second series of estimates by Newmarch are published in the sixth volume of *A History of Prices*. Here his base for the calculation is broadened by the collection of a further batch of 12,687 bills amounting to £5,254,100, which was collected in 1854. Together with the information on the bills collected in 1849, he could now analyse 17,254 bills amounting to £6,470,984. He does not, however, give full particulars of this sample of bills. He only gives the end result, i.e. the estimated amounts of inland bills drawn in England and Wales for each quarter of the years 1830–53.[4]

---

[1] T. Tooke and W. Newmarch, *A History of Prices*, Vol. 6, Appendix xi, Circulation of Bills of Exchange during each Quarter of Each of the Twenty-four Years, 1830–1853; ...

[2] Newmarch, 'An Attempt...', p. 146.

[3] These statistics are published in the following places: Secret Committee on Joint Stock Banks, 1837, *Report*, Appendix 5 (for 1828–36), BPP 1837, Vol. 14; Secret Committee on Commercial Distress, 1847–8, *Report*, Appendix 27 and 29 (for July 1829–44), BPP 1847–8, Vol. 8. I do not know where Newmarch obtained the figures for 1845–7. In his article quoted above, Newmarch writes that his data were obtained from the above two reports and for October to December 1847 from the Board of Trade, but for 1845 to September 1847 he does not disclose his source.

[4] The statistics of revenue from stamps on bills which were used in these calculations are to be found in BPP 1854, Vol. 39, p. 287 *et seq.*

As foreign bills were not assessed for stamp duty before 1854, it is impossible to make a more or less accurate estimate of the amount of foreign bills in this period. Both Leatham and Newmarch relied on their impressions in determining the proportion of the volume of foreign bills to that of inland bills. In the sample of bills collected in 1849 by Newmarch, the number of foreign bills was 834 and their total amount was £280,444 or about one-third of the total amount of inland bills. In spite of this Newmarch writes,

I am by no means sure, however, that the facts contained in the bankers' returns can be received with safety as a fair sample of the general bill circulation of the country as regards foreign bills and I prefer to adopt the conclusion of Mr. Leatham (one-sixth), because the tenor of my own general observation is most in consonance with it, and because there are other reasons in its favour,...[1]

As these other reasons, he enumerates two facts. The one is that the five banking houses from which the samples of bills were obtained show widely varying proportions of foreign bills to inland bills in their respective bill-cases, the percentages of the former to the latter being 10·5, 46·6, 17·7, 31·9 and 35·0. The other is that

In the next place, by assuming one-sixth as the proportion of foreign bills, we should have generally to assume the existence of about 17,000,000 £ as such bills, as being in circulation at one time; and as the usance of this kind of paper may be stated generally to be three months, it would follow that the amount of foreign bills drawn upon this country in the course of a year would be about 68,000,000 £—a sum which approaches near to what we know to be the value of our imports, ...[2]

In 1855, when foreign bills became liable to stamp duty, however, the amount of foreign bills drawn in the year was £310 m., while that of inland bills was £502 m. Therefore, the proportion of the former to the latter in the sample of bills in 1849, namely one-third, seems to have been a more realistic figure than one-sixth favoured by Newmarch. Nonetheless, it seems safer to say that we have no means of estimating the amount of foreign bills drawn before 1854.

In 1854 there was a radical change in stamp duty on bills of exchange. The chief alterations were: (a) foreign bills drawn out of the U.K. and payable within the U.K. came to be assessed for stamp duty at the same rate as inland bills. Also foreign bills drawn out of the U.K. and payable out of the U.K., but endorsed or negotiated within the U.K., became liable to the duty at the same rate as foreign bills drawn within the U.K. and payable out of the U.K. (The last-mentioned kind of foreign bills had been liable to the duty before 1854; the rate of duty was one-third of inland bills if they were drawn in sets of three or more, and the same as inland bills, if they were drawn singly. Leatham's and New-march's estimates of the amounts of 'inland' bills, therefore, actually

[1] Newmarch, 'An Attempt...', p. 181.   [2] Ibid.

contain some amount of foreign bills. It was not a prevalent practice, however, to draw from Britain on foreign countries.) (*b*) Bills payable on demand had formerly been assessed for stamp duty at the same rate as usance bills, but now they could be drawn on 1*d.* stamps, irrespective of the face values. Cheques are, of course, a kind of bills payable on demand, so that Leatham's and Newmarch's estimates contain the amounts of cheques. (*c*) Formerly bills having more than two months to run had been liable to a higher scale of duty than that applied to bills with less than two months of usance, but now all the bills, irrespective of usance, became subject to one and the same scale of duty. (*d*) The scale of stamp duty was completely changed and the new scale of the duty is shown in Table 7.

Because there was such a drastic change in the scale, R. H. I. Palgrave, who made the fourth attempt to estimate the amounts of bills, had to collect a new sample of bills in order to ascertain the average amount of bills on each class of stamps.[1] He collected 1,400 inland bills amounting to £648,036, probably in 1870. The results of the analysis of this sample are shown in Table 8. Unfortunately, the calculations contained here show very curious results. The average amount of bills on 10*s.* stamps is given in the table as £650·0, but 10*s.* stamps are to be used for bills in the range of £750–1,000. (As will be shown later, there are grounds for thinking that 10*s.* stamps were mainly attached to bills in the range of £900–1,000 only. This is because of the efforts to minimize the tax burden.) Similarly, the average amount of bills on 15*s.* stamps is shown to be £918·0, whereas the legal range is £1,000–1,500. The average amount of bills on 20*s.* stamps, which are to be attached to bills in the range of £1,500–2,000, is given as £1,498·1 by Palgrave. These discrepancies are puzzling and Palgrave himself does not give any explanation for them. As he uses such figures as average amounts, his results are bound to be underestimates.

At any rate, Palgrave calculates the amounts of inland bills drawn during the years 1856–70 by multiplying the numbers of each class of stamps sold by these average amounts. Then he goes on to the estimation of the amounts of foreign bills. He uses the same average amounts of each class of bills, although they are derived from a sample of inland bills. He writes,

I have, therefore, to commence with an estimate of the probable amount of all bills created on the foreign bill stamps issued in the years 1859–60 to 1870–1 inclusive. The estimate is formed on the same basis as that employed for inland bills.[2]

In forming this table I have calculated the amount of bills drawn in England on foreign countries, as bearing the same proportion to the stamps issued as the inland bills. Among these

[1] R. H. I. Palgrave, *Notes on Banking in Great Britain and Ireland, Sweden, Denmark and Hamburg; with some remarks on the amount of bills in circulation, both inland and foreign, in Great Britain and Ireland; and the Banking Law of Sweden,* London, 1873.
[2] *Ibid.,* p. 39.

foreign bills which I have observed, I have remarked that the smaller ones have been drawn rather less close to the possible limit than the corresponding inland bills. The larger foreign bills, on the other hand, have been drawn closer up to the limit. We may, therefore, on an average, take the general results as corresponding with the similar particulars of inland bills. I then estimated, as nearly as I could, as is mentioned before, the amount of bills drawn on impressed stamps; these were the bills drawn in sets of three or more. To this amount I added half as much again for bills drawn singly, as I understood from very good authority that this was about the proportion of such bills, to bills drawn in sets. Since these bills were drawn on ordinary inland stamps, I have deducted the amounts so estimated from the inland bills, and as it was probable that these bills would for the most part exceed 50 £ in value, I have in those years for which the amount of inland bills is divided into groups, deducted the amount from Group 2 and 3. The estimate of these groups of bills in Table 10 is, therefore, diminished to that extent.[1]

The amounts of bills estimated by Palgrave are shown in Table 9.

The fifth attempt at estimation was made by R. W. Barnett in 1881, in an article in the *Journal of the Institute of Bankers*. He did not make a distinction between inland bills and foreign bills, but estimated the total amount of bills drawn for the period 1858–77. This is because from 1871 the Inland Revenue Office ceased to publish the breakdown between the revenue from stamps on inland bills and that from foreign bill stamps.

Barnett's method was as follows:

We may, by an examination of actual bills drawn, determine the general ratio between the full amounts covered by the stamps and the amounts drawn upon them.

We may, on the other hand, by a consideration of the possible and probable differences upon each denomination of stamp, together with the number of such stamps sold, arrive at an estimate of the actual amounts drawn for.[2]

By the first method he found that for bills under £100 the average amounts of bills on each class of stamps was 14–26 % lower than the maximum possible amounts, while for bills for £100–£300 the former was 20–35 % lower than the maximum and for bills over £300 the difference was 2·33–5·75 %. And as the revenue from stamps under 1s. was 17 % of the total revenue from stamps on bills and that from stamps of 2s. and 3s. was 18 % of the total, he made a rough calculation as follows:

$$
\begin{aligned}
66{\cdot}66 \ @ \ 5\% &= 3{\cdot}33 \\
16{\cdot}66 \ @ \ 22\% &= 3{\cdot}66 \\
16{\cdot}66 \ @ \ 30\% &= 5{\cdot}00 \\
\hline
& 12{\cdot}00
\end{aligned}
$$

Thus, he says that by multiplying the revenue from stamps by 2,000 (the maximum rate of duty was 1s. in £100) and then subtracting from the product 12 % of it, we can estimate the amounts of bills drawn.

[1] *Ibid.*, p. 43.
[2] R. W. Barnett, 'The Effect of the Development of Banking Facilities upon the Circulation of the Country', *Journal of the Institute of Bankers*, 1881, p. 84.

His second method was to multiply the number of each class of stamps sold by the median amount of bills of that class; for example, a 9*d*. stamp was used for a bill in the range of £50–£75 and so if we know the number of 9*d*. stamps sold during a period, we can estimate the amount of bills drawn on 9*d*. stamps by multiplying the number by £62·5, the median amount. He found that the results obtained by the two methods were practically the same for the year 1876.

He then points out that the first method cannot be used without modification for the years before 1870, when the stamp duty rate for bills above £500 was not precisely 1*s*. in £100. He writes,

It is, however, probable that to some extent the difference was modified by splitting the amounts drawn for; thus £600 would most likely have been drawn in two amounts upon a 5*s*. and a 1*s*. stamp, instead of upon one for 7*s*. 6*d*. In order to make a full allowance for the difference, I have, therefore, deducted, for the years prior to 1870, 3 per cent. more, making 15 per cent.[1]

By his first method he estimated the total amounts of bills drawn for the years 1858–77. His results are shown in Table 10. If we compare Table 9 and Table 10, we can see that Palgrave's estimates are about 6 % smaller than Barnett's. As has been mentioned, it may be suspected that Palgrave's estimates are underestimates. Barnett's estimates agree with my own very well after 1870, as will appear later. But the method adopted to estimate the amounts of bills before 1870, i.e. deducting 15 % from 2,000 times the revenue from stamps, instead of 12 %, seems to lead to underestimates again. For, if, as he said, £600 was customarily drawn for in two bills of £500 and £100, stamps of 7*s*. 6*d*. must have been used mainly for bills in the range of £700–£750, so that the difference between the average amount of bills on 7*s*. 6*d*. stamps and their maximum possible amount of £750 must have been narrower than it would otherwise have been. Therefore, if the proportion of the amount of bills under £500 to the total was larger before 1870 than after (so that, if in his rough calculation quoted above the lower two multiplicands were larger in value), the multiplier in the first line must have been smaller than 5 %. It would have been better, therefore, to apply the same procedure in estimating the amounts of bills before 1870 as that used for the estimation of bills after 1870.

After Barnett, as far as I am aware, nobody attempted to estimate the amounts of bills drawn before the First World War. It is probable that, as the importance of bills in the financial market became smaller, people became less concerned with them. Contemporaries seem to have been satisfied with the rule of thumb that the volume of bills was 2,000 times the revenue from stamps.[2] In any case, the Inland Revenue Office

[1] *Ibid.*, p. 89.
[2] For example, F. Huth Jackson, in his article 'The Draft on London and the Tariff Reform', *Economic Journal*, 1904, gave the figure of £1,400 m. as the amount of bills drawn in 1902, because the revenue from stamps in that year was £700,000.

ceased to disclose the detailed statistics of stamp duties (i.e. number of stamps sold of each denomination) after 1883. As late as in 1938, *The Economist* used such rough calculation (i.e. multiplying the revenue from stamps by 2,000) to estimate the amount of bills at that time.[1]

2 ESTIMATED AMOUNTS OF BILLS DRAWN, 1855–1913

It is not always necessary to estimate the absolute amount of bills drawn in each year. If the object were to study the cyclical behaviour of the amounts of bills, for example, it might suffice to observe the movement in the total revenue from stamps on bills, for these must faithfully reflect the relative changes in the amounts of bills drawn from year to year. But unfortunately the rates of duty of stamps on bills were changed from time to time and if we want to compare the amounts of bills for two periods between which there was such a change of rate, we must calculate their absolute amounts. Moreover, it is desirable to compare the amounts of bills with other economic quantities, such as national income and bank deposits.

As has been shown in 2.1, there are two methods of estimating the amounts of bills drawn: one is to collect samples of actual bills in order to find the average amount of bills on each class of stamps and then to multiply the number of stamps sold in each year by these average amounts: the other is to assume *a priori* a median amount of bills for each class of stamps can be used as multipliers. The first method was used by Newmarch and Palgrave and is, of course, the more desirable. For the years before 1854 this is the only reasonable method, because stamp duty rates in those years were very rough in their scale and the usance of bills as well as their face values mattered in the assessment. Thus, a 5s. stamp could be used for bills in the range of from £100 (usance, more than 2 months) to £300 (usance, less than 2 months).

The second method is used by Leatham and Barnett (although both of them relied partly on the first method). This method is obviously unsatisfactory to use for the period before 1854 for the reason stated above. From 1855, however, a new scale of stamp duty rates was imposed which did not take account of bill usance and was much finer than its predecessor. For instance, a 5s. stamp was to be used for bills of £400–£500. The second method became, therefore, more realistic to employ for the estimation of bill amounts after 1855. Here the second method is used, for it is in any case impossible to adopt the first method in the twentieth century. We could, of course, use the average amounts of bills found by Palgrave, but, as has already been pointed out, there are curious aberrations among them which are likely to lead to underestimates. Moreover, the average amounts of bills on the several kinds

[1] 'Decline of the Bill of Exchange', *The Economist*, 26 March 1938, p. 689.

of stamps must change over time and it must be necessary to take fresh samples from time to time. A study of any surviving records of old established banks or merchant firms would probably be rewarding in this matter, but this attempt has not been made here.

The materials for estimation are the statistics of revenue from the sale of stamps on bills of exchange and promissory notes payable otherwise than on demand. A word of caution may be in order here. The number of bill stamps sold during a period, say a year, may not be an accurate guide of the number of bills drawn in that period. For example, firms may keep a stock of bill stamps and may draw bills on stamps bought years ago.[1] Also, two or three stamps may be attached to one bill, just as two postage stamps may be used for one letter. But clearly firms would not keep an unnecessarily large stock of stamps and the magnitude of the practice would not change much from year to year. As will be seen, the amounts of bills estimated from the yearly sale of stamps show a distinct cyclical movement which corresponds markedly well with other indices of the business cycle, suggesting that bill stamp statistics are a fairly reliable index of the amount of bills drawn in each year.

For the period 1855–79 detailed statistics giving the number of stamps sold of each denomination were published in BPP.[2] For 1880–2 the same kind of statistics were published in *The Economist*, 6 October 1883.

After 1883 these detailed statistics are not to be found anywhere. The only data available are the total amounts of revenue from stamps on bills of exchange for each financial year. These are given in the *Reports of the Commissioners for Her (His) Majesty's Inland Revenue*.

Thus, for the period 1855–82, the number of stamps sold of each class is multiplied by the median amount of bills of that class. For example, a 5s. stamp is to be attached to a bill in the range of £400–£500, so that the multiplier in this case is £450.

However, as has been quoted from Barnett, from 10 October 1854 to 31 December 1870 there was scope for avoidance of stamp duty for bills above £500. This is because the scale of the duty for bills above that amount was different from that for bills under that amount. Under £500 it was uniformly 1s. in £100, whereas for bills above that a rougher scale was applied, as will be seen from Table 7. Thus, to take an example, a transaction for the amount of £2,100 which, if drawn for in one bill, would require a 30s. stamp, could be represented by two bills of £2,000 and £100, which would use a 20s. and a 1s. stamp. Thus, 30s. stamps may have been mainly used for bills in the range of

---

[1] This was pointed out to me by Mr R. F. G. Alford of the London School of Economics.
[2] These statistics can be found in British Parliamentary Papers as follows: *Bills of Exchange and Promissory Notes*, BPP 1859, Session 2, Vol. 15, p. 253; and under *Miscellaneous Statistics of the U.K.*, for the following BPP: 1862, Vol. 60, pp. 410–11; 1864, Vol. 59, p. 162; 1866, Vol. 74, pp. 630–1; 1868–9, Vol. 62, pp. 308–9; 1872, Vol. 64, pp. 248–9; 1875, Vol. 80, pp. 546–7; 1878–9, Vol. 74, p. 402; 1882, Vol. 74, pp. 566–7.

£2,900–£3,000. This sounds quite logical and such avoidance of the tax was doubtless practised. Doubt may arise whether a saving of a few shillings on a transaction of hundreds or thousands of pounds sterling weighed so heavily in the minds of the managements of firms as to let them take the extra trouble of drawing two or three bills for one transaction. However, if we take the fourth quarter of 1870, when the old scale was in force, and the first quarter of 1871, when a new rate came into force and the reason to avoid tax disappeared, the number of stamps sold for inland bills of less than £500 increased from 1,547,832 to 1,604,188 or by 4 % between the two periods, while the number of stamps for inland bills of over £500 increased by 91 % from 59,989 to 115,228. The time was one of upswing in the business cycle, when it was probable that bills of larger denominations would have increased more than those of smaller values. Still this large difference in the percentage growth cannot be explained from the cycle alone. For, if we take the number of 5s. stamps for inland bills, it increased from 27,021 to 27,526 in the same period, whereas that of inland bill stamps of 6s.–7s. 6d. increased from 20,056 to 33,055. This means that bills of £400–£500 increased only by 2 %, while bills of £500–£750 grew by 65 %. Such a difference in the growth rates of bills of contiguous ranges of denominations can only be explained by institutional changes.

Thus, for the years 1855–70, the median amounts of bills carrying stamps above 5s. cannot be used as multipliers in estimating the amounts of bills. Instead, what could be termed minimum effective median amounts are used. For example, a 10s. stamp was for bills of £750–£1,000, so that the median amount was £875, but because of tax avoidance 10s. stamps were actually used for bills of £900–£1,000. This can be called the effective range for 10s. stamps. Then the effective median amount would be £950, but, as there were probably people careless or law-abiding enough to draw bills for £750–£900 on 10s. stamps, the minimum effective amount of £900 is used as multiplier.

There is another reason for using multipliers higher than the median amounts of bills of larger denominations. Bills of higher face values tend to be drawn in round amounts as £1,000, £2,000, £3,000 and so on. This is probably due to the circumstance that such bills were mainly drawn in connection with financial transactions. In Parliamentary Papers there is an exhaustive survey of all the stamps sold for bills during the calendar year, 1871. In this year the numbers of stamps sold of 6s. to 10s., for instance, were as follows:

6s.	55,442[1]	9s.	24,906
7s.	42,903	10s.	190,108
8s.	36,994		

[1] BPP, 1872, Vol. 36, pp. 115–17.

From this we can calculate that the average amount of bills on stamps of 6s.–10s. was £820 which was higher than the median amount of £750. From 1871 the stamp duty rate was uniformly 1s. in £100 and there was at this time no reason to avoid tax in the manner described above. Therefore, before 1870 the average amount of bills in this range must have been higher than £820.

Thus, the following amounts are used as multipliers for the estimation of the amounts of bills above £500:

Stamps	Multipliers used	Median values of bills
7s. 6d.	£700	£625
10s. 0d.	£900	£875
15s. 0d.	£1,400	£1,250
20s. 0d.	£1,900	£1,750
30s. 0d.	£2,900	£2,500
40s. 0d.	£3,900	£3,500

Bills above £4,000 raise another problem. The duty was 45s. for any bills above £4,000 until 1860 and after 1861 it was 10s. for every £1,000 or fraction of £1,000 in excess of £4,000. But the statistics of stamp duty show only the total numbers of stamps sold of 40s. or more (after 1871 the number of stamps of 50s. or more is lumped together in one column). However, from the exhaustive survey of all the stamps sold in 1871 we can calculate that the average amount of bills above £4,000 was £6,262 in that year. Therefore, £6,300 is used in multiplying the numbers of stamps of 40s. or more.

There is one more difficulty in estimating the amounts of bills before 1870. As is seen from Table 9, foreign bills which are drawn in sets of three or more can use three stamps at one-third of ordinary rates. Therefore, we must divide the numbers of these special rate stamps by three and then multiply the quotient by the median amounts of bills bearing these stamps (or by the minimum effective amounts, as the case may be). The difficulty is that the stamps of 1d., 2d., 3d., 1s., 5s., 10s., and 15s. were usable both at ordinary rates and at the one-third rates. For example, a 5s. stamp could be used for bills both of £400–£500 and of £1,000–£1,500. This does not affect the estimation of the total amounts of bills drawn. For, whether we make the calculation on the assumption that all 5s. stamps were used at the ordinary rate or that they were all used at the special rate, the results are almost the same, because on the latter assumption three times the usual multiplier is used to multiply one-third of the numbers of stamps. But if we want the breakdown of the estimated amounts of bills into several categories according to their face values, the existence of such anomalies becomes troublesome. This difficulty may be evaded, however, by classifying bills in such a manner that the double-rate stamps are embraced in the same categories: if we put bills under £75 in one class, all the bills with 1d., 2d., and 3d. stamps will be included in it, for 3d. stamps were usable for bills of £10–£25 and £50–£75: 1s. stamps were used for bills of £75–£100 and £200–£300, and bills in the range of £75–£400 are put in the same category: 5s. stamps were used for bills of £400–£500 and £1,000–£1,500 and 10s. stamps were used for bills of £750–£1,000 and £2,000–£3,000, so that bills in the range of £400–£3,000 are put in one class. This leaves the problem of 15s. stamps unsolved. They were used for bills of £1,000–£1,500 and of over £4,000 for the years 1855–60. But the number of 15s. stamps used at the latter rate is exceedingly small. Judging from the number of 13s. 4d. stamps (for bills of £3,000–£4,000), the number of 15s. stamps used at special rates must never have reached 1,000. If we divide this by three and multiply the quotient by £6,300, we get about £2 m. and that is the maximum possible error which may arise from ignoring the double character of 15s. stamps. The amount of bills in the range of £400–£3,000 may be overestimated by that amount, and bills over £3,000 underestimated correspondingly. Now in 1860 the amount of foreign bills of £400–£3,000 was estimated to be £274 m. and that of bills of over £3,000, £57 m. A maximum possible error of £2 m. may have distorted these figures by a few per cent., but no more.

The results of estimation of the amounts of bills over the period 1855–70 are shown in Table 11.

From 1 January 1871 the distinction between inland and foreign bills was abolished in regard to stamps and a new scale of duty was imposed, which is shown in Table 12. From the second quarter of the (calendar) year 1871, the Inland Revenue Office ceased to publish the breakdown between stamps sold on inland bills and those sold on foreign bills. Still, for the years 1871–82 they continued to publish the detailed statistics of the numbers of stamps sold of each amount. We can, therefore, obtain fairly accurate estimates by multiplying the numbers of stamps by the appropriate median amounts. However, the published statistics do not give the full details of the numbers of stamps above 10s. They lump together the numbers of stamps as follows: 11s.–15s., 16s.–20s., 21s.–25s., 26s.–30s., 31s.–35s., 36s.–40s., 41s.–45s., 46s.–50s., and all stamps above 50s. As has been pointed out, bills of higher denominations tend to be drawn in round amounts. Thus, we cannot use the median amount of £1,250 to multiply the number of stamps of 11s.–15s. The average amount of bills drawn on stamps of 11s.–15s. would be much higher than this median amount. I have calculated the average amounts of bills for the above classes of stamps from the exhaustive survey of stamps sold in 1871, and used them as multipliers.

These average amounts are as follows:

for stamps of	11s.–15s.	£1,300
	16s.–20s.	£1,900
	21s.–25s.	£2,300
	26s.–30s.	£2,900
	31s.–35s.	£3,300
	36s.–40s.	£3,900
	41s.–45s.	£4,300
	46s.–50s.	£4,900
	Over 50s.	£9,200

The estimated amounts of bills drawn during the years 1871–82 are shown in Table 13.

After 1882 the numbers of stamps sold of each denomination also ceased to be published. What we have is only the total amounts of revenue from stamps on bills in each financial year. In order to estimate the amounts of bills drawn from thsee total revenues, estimated amounts of bills drawn for the years 1871–82 are compared with the total amounts of revenue from stamps on bills during the same years (Table 14). It will appear from this that the amounts of bills drawn are on the average 1,787 times the revenues from stamps. Therefore, the revenue from stamps for the years 1883–1913 is multiplied by 1,790 to obtain the estimated amounts of bills drawn for these years.

From 1893 the revenue from stamps on inland bills and that from foreign bills are again separately stated (although figures for 1893–1903 are only approximate), so that we can estimate the amounts of foreign bills drawn from that year by multiplying the revenue from stamps on foreign bills by 1,790.

To be precise, there was one more amendment to the stamp duty rates in 1899. From 21 June of that year, foreign bills of exchange drawn and expressed to be payable out of the U.K. and actually paid or endorsed, or in any manner negotiated in the U.K., became subject to stamp duty at one half the rate of other bills, i.e. at 6d. per £100 of the face values of the bills. These are, of course, what are usually termed domiciled bills and their amounts do not seem to have been very great, as revenue from stamps on foreign bills scarcely decreased after 1899 in spite of the tax reduction. In any case, revenue from stamps on domiciled bills is not separately stated and there seems to be no way of allowing for this alteration in stamp duty rate.[1]

[1] This reduction in the duty was proposed by Sir Samuel Montagu. The reason was that the high rate of stamp duty was detrimental to the London money market. He said, 'I beg to ask Mr. Chancellor of the Exchequer whether he is aware that the quantity of bills of exchange drawn and payable abroad, sent here for negotiation, is greatly restricted in consequence of our stamp duty being twice as large as that imposed in France and Belgium, . . . ' (Parliamentary Debates, Fourth Series, Vol. 66, 1091–2). There is a comment on this point in Bankers' Magazine, 1899, p. 863.

Table 15 shows the estimated amounts of bills for the whole period 1885–1913.

I made efforts to estimate the amounts of foreign bills for the years 1871–82. First, the proportions of foreign bills in each of the four categories of bills (£0–£75, £75–£400, £400–£3,000, over £3,000) were calculated for the years 1855–70. Then the linear trend lines of these proportions were calculated and extended to the years 1871–82. Finally, the amounts of bills in each category were multiplied by the extended trend values of these proportions. These proportions are given in Table 16 and the estimated amounts of foreign bills in Table 17. However, such guesswork might be liable to an extremely large margin of error and so these estimates are given just as possible values and will not be used as a basis for further analysis.

The final question is to what extent these estimates can be trusted. For 1871–82 the estimated amounts of bills are on the average 1,787 times the revenue from stamps on bills, as is seen from Table 14. As the maximum rate of stamp duty is 1s. in £100 or 1/2,000 of the face values of bills, the maximum possible range of error upwards is naturally in the order of about 12 % of the estimated amounts of bills (the ratio of the estimated amounts of bills to revenue from stamps is stable over the years, ranging from 1,767 to 1,808). Since the amounts of bills for 1883–1913 are estimated by multiplying the total revenue from stamps on bills by 1,790, about the same maximum possible range of error must hold for those years, too. It is about the same for 1861–70, for during those years the estimated amounts of bills are on the average 1,782 times the revenue from stamps. For 1855–60 it must be a little larger and cannot be clearly defined, because the stamp duty for bills above £4,000 was uniformly 45s. irrespective of the denominations of bills.

Since median amounts were used as multipliers in the estimation, the maximum possible range of error downwards is also about 12%. For years before 1870, however, it is bigger than 12 %, for the multipliers applied to the number of stamps of more than 5s. are not median amounts, but minimum effective amounts, which are much higher. In order to get an idea of the maximum possible range of error downwards before 1870, an estimate was made of the amount of bills by multiplying the number of stamps sold by the minimum value of the relevant range of bills for the year 1869. The result was £1,003 m. for total bills or 21 % less than the amount estimated by median amounts and minimum effective rates.[1]

Thus, the estimated amounts of bills drawn are liable to errors of

---

[1] The minimum rate for stamps above 40s. was calculated from the exhaustive survey of all stamps sold in 1871. This gave the figure of £5,958, so that £6,000 is used as the multiplier of the number of stamps over 40s. As 1d. stamps are used for bills of £0–£5, there is no minimum value of bills on these stamps. The value of £1 was, however, used as the multiplier.

about 12 % both ways and so their first two figures only (in the case of total amounts of bills) have significance as absolute amounts. In spite of this, figures to the order of millions of pounds are given. To give figures down to millions as absolute amounts would not make sense, but as the average amount of bills drawn on each class of stamps must have some stable relationship to the median amounts and will not vary erratically from year to year, the total estimated amounts shown here, too, must have some stable relationship to the actual amounts of bills, so that the lower figures are shown as indexes of relative changes over the years in the amount of bills.

One more word of caution is necessary. As Palgrave pointed out, bills drawn in the U.K. on foreign countries were sometimes drawn on inland stamps. Palgrave thought that such bills amounted to about one half of bills drawn in the U.K. on foreign countries in sets of three or more (such bills use special rate stamps for foreign bills in sets) and estimated that they amounted to £14·5 m.–£24·5 m. during the years 1859–70, or about 3–4 % of inland bills (see Table 9). Palgrave deducted these amounts from inland bills and added them to foreign bills.[1] Such a procedure is not followed here. As there is no guarantee that such bills always amounted to about half of foreign bills in sets, it seemed better not to tinker with the statistics of stamp duties. In any case the amount of such bills is not great.

3. CONCLUSIONS

As is seen from Table 15 (or from Figure 1 which shows the identical data in a graph), the amount of bills drawn reached its peak in 1873 when the amount was £1,781 m. Then it declined until 1894 when it was £1,121 m. In the upswing of the 'Kondratieff' cycle from the middle of the nineties the amount of bills increased and reached £1,854 m. in 1913; only then was the peak of 1873 surpassed.

As for inland bills, we do not have definite data for the years 1871–92. But it is clear that their amount showed a considerable decrease both absolutely and relatively during those years. Their average amount for the ten years 1861–70 was £671 m. and, as the average amount of total bills in this period was £1,232 m., the amount of inland bills was 54 % of the total. In the ten years 1893–1902 it was £508 m. and was 42 % of the total amount (average for these ten years £1,206 m.). As far as we know, their peak was in 1864–5, when the amount was £742 m. and this amount was never reached again. (Actually their peak must have been in 1873, when their amount most probably greatly surpassed £800 m.) The nadir came in 1894 when the amount was £490 m. After that their amount hardly increased until 1905, but even

---

[1] Palgrave, *Notes on Banking*, p. 43.

thereafter the recovery was not conspicuous and even in 1913 their amount, at £651 m., was considerably below the level of 1870.

Foreign bills, on the other hand, increased substantially. Their average amount was £461 m. in 1861–70, and £698 m. in 1893–1902. Their peak in pre-1870 years was in 1870 and the amount was £647 m. In 1873 their amount may have reached upwards of £800 m. In the 1894 trough it was £630 m., so that the volume of foreign bills actually decreased during the secular downswing of the seventies and the eighties. But their recovery after 1894 was spectacular. From £630 m. in 1894 it grew to £1,203 m. in 1913. The proportion of foreign bills to the total amount of bills was 47 % in 1870, 56 % in 1893 and eventually reached 65 % in 1913.

Thus, the overall picture is that the heyday of inland bills was in the decade up to 1873, after which their amount declined till 1894 and never again reached its former peak. Foreign bills were strongly on the increase before 1873, but then their volume declined hand in hand with inland bills, though to a less extent. After 1894 their recovery far outpaced that of inland bills and the heyday of foreign bills came in the first decade of the twentieth century.

The decline of inland bills is, therefore, a phenomenon of the twenty-one years 1874–94. It may be argued, however, that prices were also falling in these years and that the decline in the volume of bills merely reflected the price trend. This is not a groundless argument. If we deflate the amount of inland bills by the Sauerbeck–Statist wholesale price index, and calculate the amount of inland bills at 1867–77 prices, it is £751 m. in 1870, £778 m. in 1894 and £766 m. in 1913. On the face of this there is no decline of inland bills. But we must also take into account the fact that the scale of the national economy grew and the volume of transactions increased. If the volume of bills is compared with these, the decline of inland bills can be viewed in a proper setting. Table 18 shows the proportion of bills to net national income calculated by Feinstein. From this it will be seen that the volume of inland bills was equivalent to 83 % of the national income on the average in the ten years 1861–70, but that it fell to 33 % in 1893–1902. It is 29 % in 1904–13, so that after 1893 there is not such a spectacular drop as during the seventies and the eighties.

Thus, from many points of view we can pinpoint the date of the decline of inland bills to the seventies and the eighties. As has been stressed in the previous chapter, the real acceleration in the bank amalgamation movement was in the nineties and the first decade of the present century. We have to look elsewhere for explanations of this decline of inland bills.

3. AVERAGE USANCE OF
BILLS

As has been mentioned, Newmarch collected information on 4,367 bills amounting to £1,216,884 in 1849. Table 5 gives the results of his analysis of these bills, according to which the average usance of inland bills is shown to be 3·4 months and that of foreign bills to be 3·2 months. But this average usance of inland bills is a simple average of the average usances of the twelve classes of bills on twelve kinds of bill stamps. This gives an erroneous idea of the real length of bill usance at the time. The true picture must be obtained by calculating the weighted average. The weighted average for inland bills in this sample is 3·9 months, that is, considerably longer than the simple average. This is because bills of larger denominations with longer usance predominate in this sample. As this sample may contain an unusually large proportion of bills of larger sums, the weighted average of usance of all the inland bills drawn in 1849 (calendar year) is attempted.

From Newmarch's sample of bills it is calculated that the weighted average of the usance of inland bills on stamps of 2s. 6d. or less is 3·0 months, that of inland bills on stamps of 3s. 6d. to 6s. is 3·7 months, and that of inland bills on stamps of 8s. 6d. or more is 4·0 months. If we apply these values of usance to the estimated amounts of inland bills in 1849,[1] the weighted average of usance of all the inland bills drawn in England and Wales in 1849 is calculated to be 3·8 months.

In the sample of 1,400 inland bills collected by Palgrave, probably in 1870 (Table 10), the weighted average of bill usance is 4·1 months. But as this sample of bills contains an unusually large proportion of bills of larger denominations (and with longer usances), the weighted average calculated from this sample is an overestimate. The average usances of bills on the several kinds of stamps in this sample are used to calculate the weighted average of usance of inland bills drawn in the U.K. in 1869. The result is 3·7 months. Thus there seems to have been no material change in the average usance of inland bills during the years 1849–69.

After Palgrave nobody seems to have attempted to make a serious study of this subject, as far as I am aware. John Dun and F. Huth Jackson made the following comments on this question. John Dun wrote in 1876, 'From inquiry and reflection, I am of opinion that the average unlapsed currency of the bills held by country banks may be

---

[1] Estimated by Newmarch and shown in *A History of Prices*, Vol. 6, Appendix II.

taken as forty-nine days.'[1] Then in 1904 F. Huth Jackson wrote that the average usance of bills was seventy days.[2]

These two opinions, however, are only based on impressions. We have to look for a more solid basis to ascertain any tendency in the average usance of bills. Such information is fortunately supplied by the balance-sheets of two banks, Parr's Bank and Liverpool Union Bank, which clarify the following items: amount of bills discounted, rebate on bills discounted and the rate of discount applied in the calculation of the rebate. From these we can calculate the number of days of unlapsed currency of bills held by those two banks.

Let x be the number of days of unlapsed currency, R the amount of rebate on bills, B the amount of bills discounted, and r the rate of discount used in the calculation of the rebate. The relationship between these is as follows:

$$Br\frac{x}{365} = R.$$

Therefore,

$$x = \frac{365R}{Br}.$$

Table 19 shows these items in the balance-sheets of Parr's Bank and Liverpool Union Bank, and the calculated days of unlapsed currency of the bills held by them. Parr's Bank gives this information from 1866 and Liverpool Union Bank from 1864. Twice the unlapsed currency calculated may give us an idea of the average usance of bills discounted by these two banks. We have to note, however, that there must have been a time gap of a few days between the drawing of the bills and the discounting. Furthermore, in the case of bills bought from bill-brokers the time lag may have been considerable. As both these banks were Lancashire banks, however, they must have belonged to the party sending bills to the London discount market for re-discount and not to the party buying bills from the market, although Parr's may have changed sides afterwards, for it became a first-class London bank in 1890. Thus, the unlapsed currency of bills discounted by the banks may tend to lead to an underestimate of the actual usance of these bills. Still the changes over time of unlapsed currency should show the tendency in the usance of bills discounted.

From Table 19 and from figure 2 (which gives the same data as those of Table 19) it is evident that the unlapsed currency of bills became shorter on the whole from the sixties to the eighties and that there was a reversal of the tendency from the late eighties to the nineties, although cyclical fluctuations sometimes blur the trend. The currency of the bills

---

[1] John Dun, 'The Banking Institutions, Bullion Reserves, and Non-Legal-Tender Note Circulation of the United Kingdom', *Journal of the Royal Statistical Society*, 1876, p. 88.
[2] F. Huth Jackson, *The Draft on London*, p. 505.

lengthened conspicuously one or two years after the collapse of the boom. Therefore, nine-year moving averages of the data are shown in Table 20 and figure 3. From these it will be seen that the unlapsed currency of bills held by Liverpool Union shortened from 56·0 days in 1868 to 48·3 days in 1883, but then it lengthened again till it became 54·1 days in 1894. In the case of Parr's Bank the unlapsed currency was reduced from 51·0 days in 1871 to 42·7 days in 1886; then it became longer again to reach 49·6 days in 1895 and afterwards declined to become 45·2 days in 1904. Since twice the unlapsed currency of bills should give us an idea of the average usance of bills, it may be said that in the early seventies the average usance of bills held by these banks was considerably in excess of three months, that it became almost three months in the middle of the eighties, but that it lengthened again and became almost three months and a half in the middle of the nineties.

It is rather surprising that such a reversal of the tendency occurred; the explanation of this will be attempted later. At this stage, however, it must be pointed out that the shortening of currency of bills from the sixties to the eighties must have been strongly influenced by the shortening of usance of inland bills, because inland bills formed the greater proportion of bills in the sixties. Or it might be thought that inland bills, which on the whole had longer usance than foreign bills, declined in quantity and the proportion of foreign bills grew, thus bringing down the average usance of bills as a whole. The average usance of foreign bills was probably much shorter than that of inland bills, as will be seen in the sample of bills collected by Newmarch, where it was 3·2 months. This was because Britain was importing on a short-term credit basis and exporting on a longer-term basis in the middle of the nineteenth century and because imports were financed by drawing of bills from overseas on Britain, while exports were financed by inland bills.[1]

On the other hand, if the average currency of bills lengthened after the middle of the eighties, it must have been due principally to the lengthening of foreign bill usance, since foreign bills must by this time have formed the major part of bills. In addition, it must be considered that these two banks were first-class institutions, so that they might

[1] *The Economist* of 9 October 1858 stated (p. 1117): 'The raw materials which we import are, as a rule, paid for either before they are shipped from the producing countries, or very soon after their arrival here. The manufactures made from them are, on the contrary, shipped to foreign markets upon long credits.' Evidence to the same effect was given before the Committee on Bank Acts, 1857 (QQ. 5143–4). Imports from and exports to the same market were done on credits of different lengths. See QQ. 1972–4, *Minutes of Evidence*, taken before the Select Committee on Bank Acts, 1857, BPP 1857 Session 2, Vol. 10. See also E. V. Morgan, *The Theory and Practice of Central Banking 1797–1913*, Cambridge, 1943, p. 157. There is also a very interesting article 'Adverse Exchanges—High Rate of Interest' in *The Economist* of 3 September 1853, p. 985. This states that British exports were done on an extremely long-term credit basis.

have been rejecting bills of longer usance before the seventies, while in the eighties and the nineties, when the shortage of bills developed, they might have tried to procure bills irrespective of their currency. If so, the movement of the currency illustrated here may lead to an underestimate of the shortening of bill usance till the eighties and an overestimate of the lengthening of it in the late eighties and the nineties.

In any case the experience of only two banks would not be sufficient to determine the overall tendency in the bill usance. There is, however, no further statistical information on this point. We have, therefore, to turn to contemporary verbal evidence. This abounds in the minutes of Parliamentary Committees and in contemporary periodicals, such as *The Economist* and *Bankers' Magazine*. In a sense this verbal evidence is more informative than mere statistics, because it touches on the various aspects of bill finance in the last century. Here a review will be attempted of the major evidence on this point in the reports of Parliamentary Committees and Royal Commissions since the beginning of the nineteenth century. This is partly for the reason that the consignment system of foreign trade had much to do with bill finance, especially with the drawing of inland bills. The decline of inland bills is closely associated with the decline of the consignment system in the latter half of the century. Hence, we have to look at the mechanism of bill finance in the earlier half of the century as a preliminary to an analysis of the shortening of bill usance and the decline of inland bills.

Two or three months seem already to have been the standard usance of domestic bills at the beginning of the nineteenth century. Before the Secret Committee on the Expediency of the Bank Resuming Cash Payments, 1819, John Gladstone, M.P. and East and West Indies merchant of Liverpool, states,

The practice in Liverpool, by which all goods are bought and sold, is that at the expiration of a given credit from ten days to three months, as may be agreed: Payments are made in bills of exchange on London, and sometimes in the acceptances of the purchaser made payable there, at dates from two to three months. Those bills form the great circulating medium of Liverpool, that they are paid and received by buyers and sellers, ...[1]

Before the same Committee two other witnesses, Lewis Loyd, a London banker, and Samuel Gurney, a noted bill-broker, gave evidence to the same effect.[2] These bills circulating from hand to hand in Lancashire were famous for their dirty appearance, because long lists of endorsements were attached to them. Even in transactions between wholesaler and retailer these bills were drawn and circulated, for they ranged in amounts 'from £5 to £5,000, £8,000 and £10,000'.[3] They may be termed the true domestic bills used in the finance of

---

[1] Secret Committee on the Expediency of the Bank Resuming Cash Payments, 1819, *Minutes of Evidence*, BPP 1819, Vol. 3, pp. 105–6.
[2] *Ibid.*, pp. 165 and 179.   [3] *Ibid.*, p. 165.

purely domestic trade, although it might be difficult clearly to define what constitutes the 'purely' domestic trade.[1]

The circulation of these bills had, however, already begun to decline in 1819. Lewis Loyd stated that '...bills of exchange under £20 have certainly, within the circle of my own connections in Manchester, been materially reduced since the last stamp duty.'[2]

Bills of exchange were not assessed to stamp duty until 1782, but subsequently increasingly high tax came to be imposed. When the tax was first imposed in 1782 it was 3*d*. for bills under £50 and 6*d*. for bills of £50 and upwards.[3] For 1815–53 the duty was as high as 1*s*. for bills under £5, if they were drawn for less than two months. For a £5 bill of two months date a charge of 1*s*. would be equal to 6% per annum interest. It is small wonder that small bills of exchange, which had formed the bulk of circulation in Lancashire, came to be replaced by bank post bills and Bank of England notes.[4]

However, the fact that the circulation of bills from hand to hand ceased does not necessarily mean that they ceased to be used as instruments for giving and obtaining credit in domestic trade. In any case such circulation of bills was a phenomenon limited to Lancashire and the West Riding of Yorkshire.

In other parts of Great Britain, too, the standard usance of inland bills was two or three months even in these early years of the century. Or rather it might be better to say that banker witnesses before the Parliamentary committees tried to stress that the standard usance of bills discounted by them was less than three months. Before the Secret Committee of 1819 Ebenezer Gilchrist, a director of the British Linen Co., said that the common date of bills the banks in Scotland discounted was less than three months.[5] Before the Select Committee on Promissory Notes in Scotland and Ireland, 1826, the following bankers testified that such was the case: John Commelin, agent to the British Linen Co. at Dumfries, Hugh Watt, cashier of the Arbroath Banking Co., John Mass, a Liverpool banker, William Birkbeck, a banker at Settle,

---

[1] Ashton has written a lucid exposition of this kind of bill in his essay, 'The Bill of Exchange and Private Banks in Lancashire, 1790–1830' in *Papers in English Monetary History*, ed. by T. S. Ashton and R. S. Sayers, Oxford, 1954.

[2] Secret Committee on Expediency, 1819, *Evidence*, p. 165.

[3] Commissioners of Inland Revenue, 1856–69, *Report*, BPP 1870, Vol. 20, pp. 500–2.

[4] Lewis Loyd told the Lords Committee of 1819, '.... It is within my knowledge, from the transactions of my own house, that the supplies of provisions which are drawn from neighbouring counties, used to be paid for in small bills of exchange, mostly of £10 or lower; but now the persons going to the neighbouring counties for supplies of provisions, take with them Bank of England Notes and Bank Post Bills, stating that the stamp is too serious an object to them to be paid on such small sums. There is hardly a day when I do not send £2,000 in Bank Post Bills for the purpose to Manchester, which we hardly ever used to do before the last addition to the stamp duty.' Secret Committee on Expediency, 1819, *Evidence*, p. 82.

[5] Secret Committee on Expediency, 1819, *Evidence*, p. 214.

Yorkshire, Arthur Guinness, a director of the Bank of Ireland.[1] It would be tedious to continue such a list, for the bankers giving evidence to Parliamentary committees in the nineteenth century were almost unanimous in saying that most of the bills they discounted had dates under three months and that, even if they occasionally discounted four or six months bills, these were exceptions to the rule.

However, when we turn to the sample of inland bills collected by Newmarch and Palgrave, we find that the average usance of bills of larger denominations was four months or more. According to Newmarch's estimate, bills of more than £300 of face value amounted to £112 m. out of the total amount of bills drawn of £222 m. in the (calendar) year 1849. In his sample bills of more than £300 have the (weighted) average usance of four months. From this we can see that so far from bills of four months' or six months' usance being exceptions they rather formed a sizeable proportion of inland bills at the time. The same can be said from Palgrave's sample of bills.

What then was the nature of these long-dated bills? There seem to have been two kinds of inland bills. Admittedly, those bills that were used in purely domestic trade must have had a currency of less than three months. If bills of larger denominations commonly had usances of more than three months, the nature of transactions behind these may have been different from purely domestic trade.

Before the Select Committee on Promissory Notes of 1826, Kirkman Finlay of Glasgow stated,

I believe great part of the business has been carried on by the manufacturer consigning his goods to an agent in South America, and in many instances receiving bills, the acceptance of the partners of that agent residing in this country, for a part of the value of the goods, some one half and some three fourths, at six months date; I believe that has been the mode; and those bills, many of the bankers have been in the habit of discounting, waiting for the returns to be made on the sales of the goods for the payment of those bills.

Supposing the returns not to be made, as obviously they could not be, within six months, in most cases, what was then the course followed by the party who had originally drawn the bills on the credit of the goods?—I believe a great many of them have been renewed....

Bills renewed for a second term of six months?—For either a second term of six months, or a shorter date, under the understanding that they must be renewed till after the return is made for the produce of the goods.

The Committee are to understand that those goods are neither sent out by merchants on their own account, nor in consequence of any orders to the manufacturer himself, to seek a market in South America?—The manufacturer of course had communications with partners of the agent in America, and understanding that those goods were likely to meet with a profitable sale in that country,....[2]

It is well known now that foreign trade till the seventies of the nineteenth century was largely conducted by the consignment system as

---

[1] Select Committee on Promissory Notes in Scotland and Ireland, 1826, *Minutes of Evidence*, BPP 1826, Vol. 3, pp. 415, 444, 487, 489, and 491–2.

[2] Select Committee on Promissory Notes, 1826, *Evidence*, pp. 318–19.

described here and so it would be superfluous to quote more evidence in an effort to reveal its nature in more detail. It may suffice here to point out the following characteristics of the system: (*a*) the export transactions gave rise to inland bills of long usance; (*b*) these bills could be renewed on maturity if the proceeds of the sale of the goods did not come back in time; (*c*) the goods were sent out on manufacturers' accounts as adventures, and not in consequence of orders.[1]

The voyage from Britain to South America and back seems to have taken at least four or five months in those days,[2] and the fact that the goods were sent out as adventures on the part of manufacturers, not in consequence of orders, means that it must have taken some time before the goods were actually sold and that, if a glut developed on the market, the time needed for the sale of goods might have been indefinitely prolonged. Moreover, the information that there was a market for the goods had been despatched five months before the goods arrived in South America. In the circumstances, the renewal of the bills was inevitable and seems to have been an integral part of the transaction. Of course more long-dated bills, say twelve months' bills, could have been used and were actually drawn,[3] but it may have looked more respectable to draw four or six months' bills with an understanding that they would be renewed on maturity. Six months' bills with agreements

---

[1] Before the Committee on Promissory Notes, 1826, John Gladstone gave the following account of changes in the mode of transacting export trade from the end of the eighteenth century, '...On my first acquaintance with that business, our exports were wholly, or almost wholly made by the regular merchant, who purchased his goods from the manufacturer; he generally sent them in certain quantities, and in regular annual supply to markets where he either had his own establishments, or where there were establishments for whom he executed orders. This system went on till about the close of the last century, when our manufacturers in improving their machinery and extending their concerns, finding the regular merchant not disposed to take off their goods in quantity such as they could create, it led to the establishment of a number of young houses, with abundance of enterprise but not much capital; and who obtained from the manufacturers credit to a very considerable extent. This system continued till 1809 or 1810, when a crisis something like the present took place, and brought a great proportion of those houses down. The manufacturers in general then (and had also previously) suffered very heavy losses by such failures, and therefore since 1810 they have become more the shippers of their goods to a foreign market for their own account, in place of selling them, as they had formerly done, to the exporting merchant; their business has since that period extended itself very considerably, and the manufacturers, that is those who have required assistance in carrying on their business, have found it in obtaining accommodation from the agency houses employed by them for the purpose of selling their goods in the foreign market; those agency houses have establishment in London or Liverpool, with branches of those establishments in the foreign ports, they accommodate the manufacturers by accepting bills drawn upon them by him to the extent of a half, in many cases two-thirds of the value of their shipments, (I believe two-thirds has been a more common proportion than any other) those bills have been at various dates, from four to six months, in particular instances longer, but four to six months have been the general dates,...' (*ibid.*, p. 475).

[2] Select Committee on the State of Commercial Credit, 1811, *Report*, BPP 1810-11, Vol. 2, pp. 2-3.

[3] Select Committee on Promissory Notes, 1826, *Evidence*, pp. 406-7.

to renew must have been more acceptable to banks than twelve months' bills without renewals: for banks could decline to discount the renewed bills on the maturity of the first bills.

Thus, the standard usance of bills could have been different from what could be termed the standard period of transactions. If we take the case of export trade with countries like India, China, Australia and the Pacific coasts of the Americas, the time needed for the transportation of the goods and the time needed for sending back the money proceeds could together have been as long as eighteen months till the thirties and as long as eight or nine months till the sixties, when such technical innovations as ocean-going steamers with compound engines, submarine telegraphs and the Suez Canal revolutionized transport and communications. In spite of this the export trades to these distant parts were financed by drawing four or six months' bills on London or Liverpool. Thus, standard usance of bills was in many instances just a fiction to rig up a semblance of respectability by which financing of these long-distance trades was made more palatable to the banks which discounted these bills.[1]

It is no wonder, then, that inland bills of larger face values had average usance considerably in excess of three months. A large proportion of them must have been inland bills drawn for the finance of export trade, while bills of smaller denominations may chiefly have been for genuine domestic trade.

On the other hand, the transactions of imported raw materials seem to have been financed by three months' bills even in the earlier part of the nineteenth century. John Gladstone told the Select Committee on Promissory Notes, 1826,

In Lancashire, bills drawn for the payment of goods in the regular course of business are at two and three months date; for cotton, which forms perhaps more than a moiety of the whole amount of the trade of the port, the bills are drawn at three months, that is the date stipulated for by the seller. I am not aware that bills of exchange in the ordinary course of business are ever drawn at a longer date than three months. We sell West India produce in Liverpool to our wholesale grocers, and take their acceptances at four months, payable in London, but these acceptances are seldom put into circulation until perhaps half of the time has been run off.[2]

That payment either in cash or in bills of less than three months was the standard practice in the transactions of raw cotton even in these

---

[1] There were some other techniques for providing such a semblance of short usance. One was to combine book credit with bill finance: i.e. the seller might wait a few months before he drew a bill on the buyer. (Evidence by John Gladstone before the Secret Committee on the Resumption of Cash Payments, 1819, Vol. 3, pp. 105–6.) Another was to draw twelve to eighteen months' bills on the export merchants to deposit them with some first-class houses and then to draw two or three months' bills on these houses. (Evidence by Thomas Richardson before the Select Committee on the High Price of Bullion, *Minutes of Evidence*, BPP 1810, Vol. 3, p. 149.)

[2] Select Committee on Promissory Notes, 1826, *Evidence*, p. 478.

early years was also testified by George Smith, cotton spinner and calico manufacturer of Manchester, before the Select Committee on Manufactures, Commerce, and Shipping, 1833:

Q.9290.   ...there are many in Manchester who still go to Liverpool to buy cotton, and sell it again to spinners.

Q.9291.   Do they give credit to the spinners?—Yes.

Q.9292.   What credit do they give?—From 14 days to three months.

Q.9293.   What is the credit of the manufacturer who buys his cotton immediately of the importer?—Ten days.[1]

Of course, one must not treat this evidence uncritically. The cash payment referred to here may be just the practice of first-class houses in the depression phase of the business cycle. However, there seems to be no evidence testifying to payment in cash or on a short-term credit basis as far as the export trade is concerned. It is well known that Britain was paying for her imports in cash or on a short-term credit basis, while she was exporting on long-term credit.[2] This must have been reflected in the short usance of bills drawn for the transaction of imported raw materials and in the long usance of bills for the finance of exports. Obviously the manufacturers who drew long-dated bills against their exports discounted them with banks in order to pay in cash for the raw materials.

The circumstances were not much different in the middle of the century. In order to ascertain what was the standard usance of bills in the middle of the century, some more evidence will be quoted from Parliamentary Committees of the period 1847–58.

(1) *Exports to the United States*

These were chiefly financed by drawing four months' bills without engagements to renew (inland bills drawn by the manufacturers on the merchants shipping the goods). Two witnesses testified to this.[3] The

---

[1] Select Committee on Manufactures, Commerce and Shipping, Minutes of Evidence, BPP 1833, Vol. 6.

[2] Imports from distant places like India and China were drawn for in long bills like ten months' date or six months' sight. But generally imports were paid for in two or three months' bills. For example, John Aston Yates, a broker of Liverpool, stated in 1823: '...Every man of business knows, that when goods are sent for sale to this country, the consignor draws in general, at two or three months date, upon the consignee (at the time when he transmits the bill of lading) for two-thirds or three-fourths of the value, these bills frequently fall due before advantageous sales can be made of the goods, or when the goods are sold, but the payments not received; the merchant then, if his stock of goods be large and his own funds are locked up, applies to his broker for a sum of money on account of the sales, or to his banker who will advance on the broker's bill or engagement to pay the same out of the proceeds as they are received.' Select Committee on the Law relating to Merchants, Agents, or Factors, 1823, *Minutes of Evidence*, BPP 1823, Vol. 4, pp. 376–7.

[3] See the following evidence: Alexander Henry Wylie, a Liverpool merchant engaged in American cotton trade and exports to America, before the Select Committee on Commercial Distress, 1847, BPP 1857 Session 1, Vol. 2, QQ.2096–9; David Barclay Chapman, managing partner of Overend, Gurney & Co., before the Select Committee on Bank Acts, 1857, *Evidence*, Q.5133.

evidence of Lawrence Robertson, cashier of the Royal Bank of Scotland, however, does not refer directly to export credit to the United States, but to bills drawn in connection with exchange operations.

I think it was more of the nature of exchange operations, affording credits to parties in New York to be operated upon by bills drawn on the Western Bank and City Bank...The two banks were in the habit of accepting four months inland bills drawn from London, Liverpool and Glasgow, in respect of these credits,...[1]

Probably money raised in this manner was sent to New York to be invested in securities, or New York banks may have drawn on Britain against the money and sold the bills at favourable rates of exchange. This presupposes, however, that four months' inland bills were customarily used in financing American trade and that British banks and bill-brokers habitually discounted them.

(2) *Imports from the United States*

Two months' bills drawn from the United States on Britain were the normal instruments of finance. Again, there is evidence in the Parliamentary reports of 1847–58.[2] The time needed for the voyage from America was more than two months, so that for British importers two months' usance was tantamount to cash payment. In order to pay for the unsold imports the following technique was resorted to:

There are two kinds of bills drawn against produce; the first is the original bill drawn abroad upon the merchant, who imports it. In consequence of the steamers, the bills which are drawn against produce frequently fall due before the produce arrives. The merchant, therefore, when it arrives, if he has not sufficient capital, has to pledge that produce with the broker till he has time to sell that produce. Then a new species of bill is immediately drawn by the merchant in Liverpool upon the broker, on the security of that produce, lodged in the warehouses in Liverpool, bonded or free....[3]

(3) *Exports to South America*

Six months' inland bills with agreements to renew were used for the finance of exports to the Pacific coast of South America.[4] As to the standard usance of bills for the exports to the other parts of Latin America there is no evidence before the Committees of this period, but James Bristow, a director of the Northern Banking Co. of Belfast, stated that bills drawn for the finance of exports to Brazil and Mexico were frequently renewed.[5]

[1] Select Committee on the Operation of Bank Acts, 1857–8, BPP 1857–8, Vol. 5, Q. 3391.
[2] Alexander Henry Wylie, before Select Committee on Commercial Distress, 1847, *Evidence*, QQ. 1972–4; David Barclay Chapman, before the Select Committee on Bank Acts, 1857, *Evidence*, Q. 5130.
[3] Evidence given by James Lister of Liverpool Union Bank before the Select Committee on Commercial Distress, 1847, *Evidence*, Q. 2512.
[4] Adam Hodgson, a director of the Bank of Liverpool, before the Secret Committee on Commercial Distress, 1847–8, *Evidence*, BPP 1847–8, Vol. 8, QQ. 37–40.
[5] Select Committee on the Operation of Banks Acts, 1857–8, *Evidence*, Q. 5276.

(4) *Exports to India*

Six months' inland bills with understandings to renew were used.[1]

(5) *Imports from India*

Imports from India had been drawn for by 10 months' date bills before 1847; since then the usance had been reduced to six months' sight (equal to eight months' date).[2]

Thus long-dated inland bills formed an essential link in the long chain of transactions from imported raw materials to the exports of manufactured products. Such a state of affairs seems to have survived until about the early seventies. This can be seen from the fact that in the sample of 1,400 inland bills collected by Palgrave those above £300 had the (weighted) average usance of 4·1 months.

During the seventies and the eighties, however, a radical change seems to have occurred. The circumstances which caused such a change and the nature of the changed system of export credit were lucidly explained by A. D. Provand, M.P., an export merchant to China and Japan, before the Gold and Silver Commission (Royal Commission appointed to inquire into the Recent Changes in the Relative Values of Precious Metals, 1886). He gave the following evidence:

Q. 3253. Now, suppose that in the year 1873, before the fall in silver began, you sent out a shipment of cotton goods to Shanghai?—I bought an invoice of cotton goods in Manchester, and shipped it off. I drew on London for the amount of that invoice at six months, and if the proceeds had not returned from China within the six months, I had the bill renewed for, say, three months. By that time the proceeds of these goods would be back again in my possession. *Q. 3260.* ...It was in 1876 that the great alteration in the method of financing shipments were made, and then a large number of those who traded to the East instead of drawing on London became so frightened about the fall in silver that they drew on Shanghai in taels, or on Hong Kong or on Japan in dollars, as the case might be. The shipper would draw a bill on Shanghai at 60 days, which a bank in London would buy at a rate of exchange they (the banks) fixed themselves, and this saved him from any further risk of a fall in the exchanges. *Q. 3262.* But on the renewal?—There could be no renewal of such a draft in this country, because this draft went out of the country.... in 19 cases out of 20 the bill of lading and the policy of insurance would be attached to the draft when it was handed into the office of the bank here in London. *Q. 3264.* ...There are still some merchants who draw in Manchester on London. There are two ways in which it is done. He may draw on London and run his risk of the exchange, awaiting till the proceeds came home. *Q. 3265.* That is a method which has been given up?—To a large extent. The other way is often done. He draws

---

[1] John Horsley Palmer, before the Select Committee on Commercial Distress, 1847, *Evidence,* Q. 897; Charles Turner, a merchant of Liverpool, before the Secret Committee on Commercial Distress, 1847–8, *Evidence,* Q. 810; William Patrick Paton, a Glasgow merchant, *ibid., Evidence,* QQ. 7778–80; David Barclay Chapman, before the Select Committee on Bank Acts, 1857, *Evidence,* Q. 5138.

[2] Charles Turner, before the Select Committee on Commercial Distress, 1847, *Evidence,* QQ. 853 and 856; Robert C. L. Bevan, a London banker, before the Secret Committee on Commercial Distress, 1847–8, *Evidence,* QQ. 2349–52; William Patrick Paton, *ibid.,* QQ. 7782–3, QQ. 7823–4; James Morris, *ibid.,* Q. 2767.

on London for the sake of getting cheap money, and at the same time telegraphs to his correspondent in Shanghai to buy forward as much exchange in sterling as the proceeds of the goods will amount to, thus ensuring himself a certain return for the goods when the proceeds came home. This is done to an enormous extent with India, but to a smaller extent with China, on account of difficulties which I will by-and-by point out. *Q.3273.* . . . There is no forward business with Shanghai, or very little. As the produce business from India enables the banks to buy bills on London 'forward', they in turn sell their own bills on London 'forward', chiefly as remittances for proceeds of imports sold in India. They thus obtain 'cover' transactions, and as the sale on India by the India Council of 14 millions per annum to a large extent controls the rate of exchange, competition is created between the banks, and under ordinary circumstances, in a free market, the Indian banks cannot obtain a rate of exchange that will cost the merchant more than, say, 6 per cent. per annum for the use of their money on a draft sold to a bank in London against a shipment of manufactured goods to India. . . . All the before-mentioned conditions are wanting in the trade with China and Japan.[1]

Although Provand ascribed the main cause of the change to the fall in silver prices, such a drastic shortening of usance from six months (if we consider the renewal, nine months) to two months would not have been possible without the Suez Canal, steamers and telegraphs.

As Provand said, there were still merchants who drew from Manchester on London against shipments to India. These used to be six months' bills, as has often been mentioned above. This long usance was taken up in correspondence to *The Economist*, 1 February 1879:

But the time may also have come for a change in the mode of financing for goods shipped from this side to our India and China market. The long inland bills at six months' date that hitherto have been the means by which outward shipments have been worked, are no longer needed, now that goods can reach their determinations easily within two months by the Suez Canal, and the proceeds can be returned immediately after by telegraphic transfers. An inland bill at three months would, therefore, also be ample for this branch of the trade.[2]

It seems that by 1881 four months became the standard usance in this kind of bills. There is further correspondence in *The Economist*, 1881:

As regards outward business, a Manchester buying agent will draw at four months' date on his London correspondents, who require all the time to get home the proceeds by letter, though by telegraphic transfers they may have three weeks to spare. If we reckon the voyage to Calcutta five weeks, unloading and reloading one week, time allowed purchaser six to eight weeks, and homeward mail three weeks, the four months are exhausted.[3]

This letter was written in protest at the move to shorten the usance still further to three months and so was from an interested party, but the fact that even this writer did not insist that six months were the appropriate length of bills shows that six months' bills were not customarily used any more.

There was a corresponding move to reduce the standard usance of

[1] Royal Commission appointed to inquire into the Recent Changes in the Relative Values of Precious Metals, *First Report: Minutes of Evidence*, BPP 1887, Vol. 22.
[2] Correspondence by 'Exchange', *The Economist*, 1 February 1789, p. 124.
[3] Correspondence by 'An Indian Merchant', *The Economist*, 1 January 1881, p. 13.

bills drawn from the Far East and India on Britain. Already in 1866 in the wake of the Overend, Gurney crisis, *The Economist* had written,

The crisis of 1847 enabled the banking and mercantile community of that time to reduce the India and China usance from ten months' date to six months' sight, and the lapse of twenty years with all the acceleration of speed and establishment of telegraphs certainly justifies, or rather renders necessary, such a further reduction as is now proposed.[1]

The proposal was that the usance should be reduced to four months' date. *The Economist* thought this reduction was necessary, as people without capital went into the India trade because of the long usance. 'They pay for the goods in India by the proceeds of the bill which they draw against them and their correspondent on this side provides for the bill by selling or pledging the goods, assuming the English market to be favourable and to leave any margin in the operation.'[2]

This proposal of *The Economist* brought forward some letters of protest from India merchants.[3] They stressed that the transportation of goods from India to London took four months and that, until the sale of the goods was effected, six to ten months after shipments from India were necessary. Although six Indian banks (five Anglo-Indian banks and Comptoir d'Escompte de Paris) agreed not to buy or sell bills with terms exceeding four months' sight (equal to five months), this move seems to have been a little premature. The banks apparently did not adhere to the agreement, for the same move was made again in 1878–80. *The Economist* in 1878 wrote again on this point,

But with the introduction of steam and fast sailing clipper ships, the need for such a long credit was removed, and by the subsequent opening of the Suez Canal the conditions of business have been so changed that long bills are now not only unnecessary, but positively mischievous. They afford dangerous facilities for reckless financing, for, as transactions with China can now be readily enough completed within three months, the employment of six months' bills enables a trader to have the use of money for several months after the goods, which constituted the security for the advance, have passed out of his possession.... Goods have been shipped to or from this country, not with a view of realising a profit upon their sale, but simply as a means of raising money.[4]

Thus, in February 1879, the five Anglo-Indian banks and Comptoir d'Escompte once again agreed among themselves to shorten the standard usance of Eastern bills to four months' sight.[5] This decision

---

[1] *The Economist*, 16 June 1866, p. 700.
[2] *The Economist*, 16 June 1866, p. 700.
[3] 'Usance of Indian Bills' by 'An East India Merchant', *The Economist*, 30 June 1866, p. 770; 'Usance of Indian Bills' by 'An East India Banker', *The Economist*, 7 July 1866, p. 798.
[4] *The Economist*, 9 November 1878, p. 1315. The same argument is put forward in *The Statist*, 9 November 1878, 'Bank Acceptances'; 'Bills in the Eastern Trade' (a correspondence by 'Dissector'), *ibid.*, 7 December 1878; 'Bills in the Eastern Trade' (a correspondence by 'X'), *ibid.*, 7 December 1878. W. Rathbone of Liverpool, too, expressed the same opinion in his letter to *The Economist*, 25 January 1879, p. 94.
[5] *The Economist*, 1 March 1879, p. 234.

was, however, reversed in 1882. In April of that year the Anglo-Indian banks decided to accept and discount bills with longer usance than four months. According to *The Economist* the reason was,

The shorter usance, it was stated, was, in a manner, forced upon certain of those institutions by the London banks, who refused to re-discount bills with more than 4 months to run; but as other of the Indian banks, who had not been similarly coerced, took 6 months papers, those who attempted to restrict themselves to 4 months' bills believe they have suffered in the competition.[1]

Probably this is because banks were experiencing a great scarcity of bills and Anglo-Indian banks as well as London banks were only too eager to discount six months' bills, even those with the character of finance bills. In any case six months' Eastern bills lingered on until the first decade of the twentieth century. Sir Felix Schuster of the Union of London and Smiths Bank told the National Monetary Commission of the United States, 1910, as follows:

Q. Are such bills [bills accepted by the bank] usually drawn at not to exceed ninety days?—A. That depends entirely on the usage of the country where they are drawn....In some countries they go to three or four months, and in the Far East to six months, but Far Eastern bills are getting shorter. The longer period was applied for sailing vessels, but these are going out of use, and the bills have got shorter. There is nothing beyond six months.[2]

But, in any case, six months had not been the standard usance since the eighties. Exports to India and the Far East were financed by drawing two or three months' bills directly on the importers or by drawing four months' inland bills on London. The imports were financed either by four months' sight bills or by six months' (probably date) bills. This reduction of the standard usance seems to have come about after 1873.

The case of Eastern bills is an extreme one, in that the most conspicuous reduction in the time needed for carriage of goods occurred here because of the Suez Canal (opened in November 1869). But submarine cables and steamers with compound engines must have been operating to reduce the standard period of transactions in other routes, too. Davis and Hughes found that the average tenor of bills bought by Nathan Trotter of Philadelphia was about sixty days before 1867, but then it was shortened to about ten days during the years 1867–82, and that thereafter sight drafts became predominant.[3]

As is pointed out in the essay, the bills were bought by Trotter as a means of remittance to Britain and not as investments. Where bills were used as instruments of financing foreign trade, there may not have been such a drastic reduction of usance as from sixty days to nil (cable

---

[1] *Ibid.*, 22 April 1882, p. 472.
[2] National Monetary Commission, 1910, *Interview on the Banking and Currency Systems: Interview with Sir Felix Schuster*, p. 38.
[3] L. E. Davis and J. R. T. Hughes, 'A Dollar-Sterling Exchange, 1803–1895', *Economic History Review*, 2nd Ser., 1960, p. 59.

transfers). Still, if cable transfers came to be used for remittances of money proceeds of the sale of British exports to the United States, the usance of inland bills drawn for the finance of such exports would be halved. As has been mentioned, in the middle of the nineteenth century the standard usance of inland bills drawn for the finance of exports to the United States was four months, while that of bills drawn from the United States on Britain was two months. If the standard usance of the latter kind of bills became nil, that of the former would become two months. Thus, the long usance of inland bills drawn for the finance of export trade became a thing of the past by the eighties. Even the standard usance of bills for the finance of exports to India became four months by the eighties.

As we have seen, the average usance of inland bills in 1869 was probably 3·7 months. If we suppose that the average usance of foreign bills in that year was three months, the weighted average of usance of all the bills in 1869 was 3·4 months.

In 1870 the nine-year moving average of unlapsed currency of bills held by the Liverpool Union Bank was 54·8 days, while that of bills held by Parr's Bank was 50·8 days. If twice these figures were the average usance of bills held by them, it was 3·7 months for the former and 3·4 months for the latter. These figures agree very well with the 3·4 months calculated for total bills in 1869. In 1883 the nine-year moving average was reduced to 48·3 days for Liverpool Union and 44·6 days for Parr's. Therefore the average usance was reduced to 3·2 months and 3·0 months respectively. Since the average usance of foreign bills seems always to have been close to three months after the middle of the nineteenth century (it was 3·2 months in the sample of bills collected by Newmarch in 1849), it was most probably the reduction in the usance of inland bills that brought about the shortening of unlapsed currency of bills held by the two banks. If we suppose that the average usance of inland bills was reduced from 3·7 months in 1869 to 3·0–3·2 months in 1883, this will mean that the amount of inland bills outstanding at one time was diminished by some 14 % on this account.

We do not know the amount of inland bills in 1883. But if we suppose that the average usance of inland bills was still 3·0 months in 1894, it may tentatively be supposed that the amount of inland bills outstanding at one time in that year was approximately £123 m. (the estimated amount of inland bills drawn in 1894 was £490 m.). The amount of inland bills drawn in 1869 was £656 m. and so the amount of inland bills outstanding was £205 m. on the assumption that the average usance was 3·7 months. Thus there was a considerable reduction in the amount of inland bills outstanding between these two dates. Both 1869 and 1894 are in the depression phases of major cycles, so that the magnitude of reduction shown here does not seem to be exaggerated.

If we take 1873 as the starting point, the reduction would appear to be much more severe, as the amount of inland bills drawn in that year appears to have been close to £900 m.

Moreover, if we consider the supply of inland bills in the London discount market, the decrease may have been much more pronounced than the above figures would suggest. Most of the bills coming to the London discount market would have been bills of larger denomination. As has been pointed out, inland bills of large denomination had a longer usance than those of smaller face values. The average usance of bills of more than £300 was 4·1 months in the sample of inland bills collected by Palgrave. The longer usance of this class of bills must have been due to the inclusion of long-dated inland bills drawn for the finance of exports, for such bills must have had bigger face values. As the shortening of usance after 1870 must have been most conspicuous among these bills, the reduction in the supply of inland bills in the London discount market must have been correspondingly greater than is explained from the shortening of usance of total inland bills. If we suppose that bills of bigger denominations than £300 had formed the bulk of supply of bills in the market, and that their usance shortened from four months to three months during the seventies and the eighties, we might estimate that the supply of inland bills to the market was diminished by some 25 % on this score.[1]

The next question is why the average usance of bills held by Liverpool Union Bank and Parr's Bank lengthened again after the latter half of the eighties. This is a surprising development, of which I had not been aware until the unlapsed currency of bills held by the two banks was calculated. In the contemporary issues of financial magazines there seems to be no mention of such a phenomenon. However, since two banks of first class rank show an identical tendency in this, the phenomenon cannot be dismissed as accidental.

First of all, it must be pointed out that this lengthening of bill tenor must be due to the longer currency of foreign bills, since they formed the bulk of bills by this time. Secondly, this cannot be associated with

---

[1] The technical changes that brought about the shortening of usance seem to have been particularly accelerated from the latter half of the sixties. The first long-distance submarine cable was that between Britain and North America and it was laid in 1866. The Suez Canal was opened in 1869. Steamers had long ago appeared on the ocean and were already in practical use as mail packets and passenger liners. But their predominance in inter-continental trade, especially of bulk cargoes, had to await the compound engine, which was re-invented in 1854 by John Elder, but the general adoption of which belonged to the post-seventies period. Compound engines and later triple and quadruple expansion engines more than halved the coal consumption per indicated horse power per hour, which was more than 4 lb. in simple engines, and long voyages without coaling were made possible by them. (See Henry Fry, *The History of North Atlantic Steam Navigation*, London, 1896, pp. 46–7. Also R. Knauerhase, 'The Compound Steam Engine and Productivity Changes in the German Merchant Fleet, 1871–1887', *Journal of Economic History*, September 1968.)

any lengthening of the standard period of trade transactions, which must still have been shortening. Therefore, the inference is that it must have been due to longer tenor of finance bills.

For such a supposition there is some ground in the fact that the currency of bills lengthened in the nineties when there developed an extreme scarcity of bills in the market. Banks and bill-brokers were then particularly eager to procure bills to discount. Hence, the market rate of discount was lowered to an extreme extent in the mid-nineties.

The market discount rates of three months' bills and six months' bills during the nineties are shown in Table 30. From Table 30 it is evident that the discount rate of six months' bills was higher than that for three months' bills when the general level of interest rate was low, and *vice versa*. Such behaviour of discount rates can be explained only from the operation of finance bills. When the general level of interest rates was low; banks and bill-brokers would have been ready to discount six months' bills. Foreigners who wanted to tap cheap money in London would have wished to draw six months' bills on London and discount them there, for a six months' bill would have ensured the use of cheap money for six months. Therefore, more six months' bills would have been drawn, which meant that the supply of such bills was greater, so that their discount rate would have been higher than that of three months' bills.

On the other hand, when the general level of interest rates was high, more three months' finance bills would be drawn than six months' bills, for it would be disadvantageous to get money on six months' bills and pay the high rate for six months, during which time interest rates might come down.

Such a relationship between the two kinds of discount rates is inconceivable where bills were drawn for the finance of real transactions. In a boom when the expected rate of profit and the general level of interest rates were both high, more six months' bills might be created in order to secure the use of money largely irrespective of the cost of money. In such a situation the discount rate of six months' bills would be higher than that of three months' bills. That such was the case before the seventies when most of the bills were for the finance of trade will be suggested in Chapter 6.

We have evidence in *The Economist* that foreign finance bills were increasing in the nineties and afterwards, but as for their tenor there is scarcely any comment there. For example, in 1895 when the London money rate was extremely low, there was a large increase in finance bills drawn from the Continent. *The Economist* of 12 October records,

London discount houses and banks have for some time past been watching quietly, but closely, the rapid increase which has been taking place in the number of continental finance bills offered to them for discount, mostly from French sources,... Nothing, of course, could be more pleasing to a foreign bank than to advance money to its customers at high rates and to recoup itself handsomely by drawing on London and getting the paper discounted at the low rates prevailing there,...[1]

In the first decade of the twentieth century American finance bills seem to have come to London in increasing quantities. The first mention of them appears in *The Economist*, 6 September 1902.[2]

Moreover, county councils and municipal corporations began to issue bills in the London market. For instance, in 1897 the London County Council issued £600,000 of six months' bills.[3] Such bills were regarded as ordinary promissory notes.[4]

We have no direct evidence to associate the lengthening of bill currency of the two banks with finance bills, but if the general tenor of bills became longer in the nineties, this seems to be the only explanation possible. For there is no reason to suppose tha the average usance of commercial bills (this term is used here to denote that the bills were drawn for the finance of actual trade) lengthened in the nineties.

It is possible, however, that the general currency of bills did not lengthen, and that only the average tenor of bills discounted by the two banks became longer. As these two banks were first-class institutions, they might have been able to preempt the short supply of bills in the depression phase of the cycle, while during the boom they rejected bills of longer usance.

[1] 'London Bankers and French Finance Bills', *The Economist*, 12 October 1895, pp. 331–2.
[2] 'London Bankers and French Finance Bills', *The Economist*, 6 September 1902, p. 1380.
[3] *Ibid.*, 22 May 1897, p. 737.
[4] *Ibid.*, 5 June 1897, p. 812.

4. RE-DISCOUNTS OF BILLS
BY LOCAL BANKS[1]

King points out that

This decline [in inland bills] may be said to have begun shortly after the 1857 crisis, although it was not until the seventies that it became at all marked. Its first cause, in point of time, was the diminution of country bank re-discounting, the abuse of which had caused so much distress, and attracted so much censure, in 1857 that regular re-discounting came to be regarded as the practice of only second-rate banks. The larger provincial banks therefore sought to avoid it at all normal times, and were enabled to do so, without seriously contracting their turnover, by the rapid growth of the banking habit and by the competitive effectiveness of their deposit allowances, which rendered bank deposits simply an alternative means of private investment. By 1875, the Liverpool banks, which, by reason of their preponderantly industrial connections, had formerly been the largest re-discounters, were regularly very large lenders in the London market, and re-discounting was 'practically never done'. The decline of bank re-discounting did not, of course, necessarily involve a reduction in the total supply of domestic paper, but it did involve a reduction in the quantity sold in Lombard Street.[2]

King bases his opinion on evidence taken before the Select Committee on Banks of Issue, 1875,[3] and on an address given by William Fowler, a well-known banker, before the Institute of Bankers in 1891.

King's opinion on this point was justified, but he did not attempt to quantify his argument. Further, it is doubtful whether the practice of re-discounting by county banks declined as early as 1857. His opinion is based on the following passage in the address by William Fowler:

After the panic of 1857 was over, I remember particularly well there was a great change in the management of the banks all over England, and I knew it in this way: The great business of our house about 1857 was re-discounting for country banks. That business rapidly reduced after 1857, because banks felt the imprudence of having such a mass of bills that they could not hold themselves, and therefore they kept more money in London than they previously had had. But that process went on far more rapidly after 1866...Those lessons have never been forgotten, and the great banks in the country that were large (re-)discounters in 1866 are now large depositors in London.[4]

We have nothing to refute this, but it was usual in the middle of the nineteenth century for the supply of bills from industrial counties to increase during a boom and to dry up during a depression. Therefore, if the amount of bills coming to London for re-discount declined after the 1857 crisis, it would be no proof that there was a secular or structural

---

[1] The research in relation to Chapters 4 and 5 has been facilitated by a grant from the Central Research Fund of the University of London.

[2] King, *History of the London Discount Market*, pp. 271–2.

[3] Select Committee on Banks of Issue, 1875, *Minutes of Evidence*, BPP 1875, Vol. 9, QQ.5285, 7171.

[4] 'Inaugural Address by William Fowler', *Journal of the Institute of Bankers*, 1891, p. 618.

change in domestic finance. Moreover, the amount of inland bills drawn was strongly on the increase after 1855.

We have no means of knowing the amount of re-discounted bills as a whole, but two banks in Liverpool, Liverpool Commercial Banking Co. and North-Western Bank, disclosed the amount of their contingent liabilities on re-discounted bills. The former disclosed these data for 1861–72, and the latter for 1864–75. The main items of their balance-sheets for these periods are shown in Table 21. (Admittedly, these two banks were not first-class banks, such as the Manchester and Liverpool District Bank, but neither were they disreputable third-class institutions. In 1873 there were seven joint-stock banks with head offices in Liverpool. Of these, Bank of Liverpool, Liverpool Union Bank and North & South Wales Bank each had deposits of more than £2 millions—Bank of Liverpool did not publish its balance-sheet and its deposits are unknown, but its paid-up capital of £625,000 was the biggest of the seven. Liverpool Commercial and North-Western had deposits of about one million, while National Bank of Liverpool held £721,000 and Adelphi Bank only £178,000 of deposits.)

From the balance-sheets of these two banks it will be seen that the amount of re-discounts experienced markedly cyclical fluctuations. During the boom of 1864–6 Liverpool Commercial Banking Co. had re-discounts of £332,000 on the average, while its discounted bills on hand averaged £636,000, i.e. it re-discounted about one-third of the bills it acquired. In the next boom of 1871–3 its re-discounts averaged £147,000 and its discounted bills on hand £841,000. In this period, therefore, it re-discounted about 15 % of its bills. (In 1871–3 it looks as if the bank practised window-dressing, for its re-discounts invariably shrank in the balance-sheets of 31 December, compared with the figures of 1 August. Here, however, both the figures of 31 December and 1 August are used to calculate the average.)

North-Western Bank did not disclose the amount of discounted bills, but it showed the amount of liabilities on bills in circulation, which probably referred to re-discounted bills. In 1864–6 these averaged £541,000, while the bank's advances and discounts averaged £1,116,000. In 1871–3 liabilities on bills in circulation were £199,000 and advances and discounts £1,169,000. Here, too, there was a relative as well as absolute decline in the amount of bills re-discounted.[1] On the other hand, cash on hand and at call increased from an average of £78,000 to £128,000. (In the case of Liverpool Commercial cash on hand and at

---

[1] Bills re-discounted of this bank suddenly increased to £481,000 on 31 December 1875. This was probably due to a minor crisis occasioned by the failure of Sanderson & Co., bill-brokers, with liabilities of £7 m. and of Aberdare Iron Co. This caused a chain reaction of stoppages, and some fairly big merchant firms, including Alex Collie & Co. failed. See *The Economist*, 5 June and 19 June 1875.

bankers showed no increase as the average of 1864–6 was exactly the same as that of 1871–3 at £118,000.)

The experiences of the two banks as to re-discounts agree very well, so that we can probably say that the amount of bills sent to London for re-discount from Liverpool in 1871–3 was not so great as it was in the boom of 1864–6. What caused this change? King suggests that the accumulation of savings deposits by Liverpool banks was one cause of this development. In the case of Liverpool Commercial Banking Co. it might well have been that the bank absorbed more savings deposits and thus became better able to hold the bills to maturity. Its average deposits in 1864–6 were £662,000 and in 1871–3 they were £976,000, in other words the deposits grew by 47 %, compared with 1864–6. On the other hand, the total sum of its loans, discounts and re-discounts was £1,400,000 in 1864–6 on average, while it was £1,481,000 in 1871–3. Thus the growth of deposits far outpaced that of loans and so on.

This bank, it may be noted, was a typical unit bank without branches until it was absorbed by Bank of Liverpool (later Martins Bank) in 1888. Thus, the augmentation in deposits of this bank was not the result of any amalgamations or of new branches in some residential areas.

In the case of North-Western Bank the average deposits were £825,000 in 1864–6 and £828,000 in 1871–3. Thus there was no growth in the deposits. But if we take the total amount of loans and discounts and liabilities on bills in circulation, it was £1,657,000 in 1864–6 and £1,368,000 in 1871–3, so that there was a decline in the lending business of the bank and in spite of this the deposits did not decrease. North-Western Bank, too, was without any branches since its foundation in 1864 (actually the conversion into a joint-stock bank of a private bank, Moss & Co. of Liverpool) till 1882 when it opened its first branch at Bootle.

In order to see whether such developments were common to other Liverpool banks, the main items in the balance-sheets of three other banks, Liverpool Union Bank, National Bank of Liverpool and Adelphi Bank, are shown in Table 22. The most conspicuous change can be seen from the balance-sheets of Liverpool Union Bank. Its average deposits were £1,708,000 in 1864–6 and £2,522,000 in 1871–3, so that they grew by 48 %. (This, too, was a unit bank until 1879.) On the other hand, the average loans and discounts increased from £2,022,000 to £2,429,000 during the same period or by 20 %. (If we take bills discounted only, they increased from £1,713,000 to £2,158,000 or by 26 %.) Cash on hand and at call showed a spectacular growth of 196 % from £265,000 to £786,000. Since most of the increase in cash on hand and at call would have been employed as money at call with London brokers, this bank had become a lender in Lombard Street by this time.

But in 1864–6 the bank was probably still a re-discounter of bills, for the amount of loans and discounts exceeded deposits by a large margin.

The balance-sheets of National Bank of Liverpool exhibited roughly the same movement as those of North-Western Bank. In 1864–6 the average deposits were £1,044,000, loans and discounts £1,302,000 and cash on hand at bankers £133,000. In 1871–3 deposits were £830,000, loans and discounts £1,035,000 and cash on hand and at bankers £253,000. Thus, both deposits and loans and discounts decreased by 20 %, but the amount of cash on hand and at bankers (which probably included money at call) increased by 90 %. This increase in cash etc. was facilitated by the increase in paid-up capital from £300,000 to £450,000 which was to be paid in October to December 1866. (In fact, part of the payment seems to have been delayed until the full amount of paid-up capital was reached in 1872.) National Bank of Liverpool opened its first branch in 1871 and the second in 1874. The accounts of Adelphi Bank showed about the same changes as those of National Bank of Liverpool and North-Western Bank. Comparing 1871–3 with 1864–6, the average deposits decreased from £206,000 to £198,000, or by 4 %; loans and discounts declined from an average of £315,000 to an average of £256,000, or by 19 %, and cash on hand and at call increased from £22,000 to £34,000, or by 55 %. In this case, too, there was an increase of paid-up capital from £104,000 to £130,000 in 1869–70. The number of offices was unchanged at 2 both in 1864–6 and in 1871–3.

Thus there is a broad similarity in the movement of accounts of banks. Either deposits increased far more than loans and discounts, or loans and discounts decreased far more than deposits. Except for Liverpool Commercial Banking Co. the amount of cash on hand and at call (or at bankers) increased substantially. Probably, therefore, the amount of bills sent to London for re-discount was smaller in 1871–3 than in 1864–6, while the amount of money sent from Liverpool to London increased during the period.

After 1875 no bank disclosed the amount of re-discounts, but judging from the balance-sheets of Liverpool Union and Liverpool Commercial, which disclosed the amounts of discounted bills, probably they did not re-discount bills in the next boom of 1880–2. During the period the discounted bills of Liverpool Commercial Banking Co. averaged £630,000, compared with an average of £841,000 in 1871–3. Deposits averaged £976,000, which was exactly the same as the average for 1871–3. Cash on hand and at call increased considerably from £118,000 to £306,000.

Liverpool Union Bank's deposits averaged £2,465,000 in 1880–2, which was smaller than the average of £2,522,000 during the preceding boom. However, the discounted bills decreased by 26 % from an average of £2,158,000 to £1,588,000, while cash on hand and at call declined from an average of £786,000 to £560,000.

Thus bills sent to London for re-discount seem to have decreased after the 1866 crisis and probably this practice came to an end in the latter half of the seventies. Country banks therefore apparently came to hold bills discounted until maturity. If this were so, local banks as a whole might well have come to hold an increasing share of the decreasing volume of inland bills, but this is almost impossible to confirm.

There are, however, four endeavours by contemporaries to estimate the amount of bills discounted by banks. These efforts necessarily involved the building of estimates upon estimates, so that they are liable to large margins of error. They are, in fact, little more than intelligent guesses. Still, if these estimates showed results inconsistent with the above supposition, we should need to have second thoughts on the reasoning. In this negative way they may be of use to us.

The first estimate was made by John Dun for the year 1874 and the next was made by James Dick for 1883. As has been mentioned, the practice of re-discounting probably came to an end between these two dates. These estimates tried to ascertain the amounts of the main items of assets and liabilities of all the banks in the U.K., but, since we are concerned here only with the discounted bills of local banks (including Scottish and Irish banks), only that portion of their work that hinges on this point will be quoted.

Dun[1] began by estimating the amount of total liabilities of country banks in 1874. For provincial joint-stock banks he employed the following four methods to estimate the amount of liabilities to the public:

(A) 49 provincial joint-stock banks published their balance-sheets; their paid-up capital amounted to £11·94 m., and liabilities to the public (= deposits + note − issues + acceptances) to £81·40 m. Of the remaining 47 provincial joint-stock banks 44 disclosed the amounts of paid-up capital which was £7·42 m. If their liabilities to the public bore the same proportion to paid-up capital as the 49 banks above, they should be £50·60 m. Three banks which did not publish their paid-up capital were small banks whose liabilities to the public were unlikely to have exceeded £1 m. in aggregate.

(B) The 49 banks publishing their balance-sheets had 549 offices. 47 other banks had 274 offices, or 5¾ per bank. Of the 49 banks those with less than 6 offices had £400,000 of liabilities to the public per office. 7 large banks without branches were, however, included among them. If they are excluded, the amount per office was £270,000. Dun quite arbitrarily reduced this amount to £250,000, and multiplied this by 274 to obtain the liabilities to the public of 47 banks of £68·00 m.

[1] John Dun, 'The Banking Institutions, Bullion Reserves and Non-Legal-Tender Note Circulation of the United Kingdom', *Journal of the Royal Statistical Society*, 1876, pp. 109–13.

(C) From the liabilities to the public of £81·40 m. of the 49 banks, £31·90 m. of the 5 largest banks are deducted, and we have the amount of £49·50 m. for 44 banks, or £1·13 m. per bank. At the same rate the liabilities to the public of the 47 banks would be £53·00 m.

(D) The Select Committee on Banks of Issue, 1875, sent question-naires to all the banks in the U.K. and asked about the volume of their deposits. Of the 96 provincial joint-stock banks 88 gave answers and their deposits totalled £119,762,000, or £1,361,000 per bank. At the same rate the deposits of the remaining 8 banks would be £10,890,000. The note-issues of English joint-stock banks in 1874 were £2,276,000 and acceptances were £2,100,000 (partly estimated); the total liabilities to the public of these 96 banks were £135,028,000.

As the total liabilities to the public estimated by the four methods above agree very well, Dun put the amount as £134·0 m.

For provincial private banks Dun estimated their total liabilities to the public by the following three methods:

(A) 49 provincial joint-stock banks had liabilities to the public of £81·40 m. and the number of their offices was 549, as was stated above. The amount per office, therefore, was £148,000. Dun thought that the amount per office of private banks was a little more than this and £160,000 was thought to be the appropriate amount. As the number of offices of provincial private banks in 1874 was 523 (196 banks), the total liabilities to the public would have been £84·0 m.

(B) With 36 joint-stock banks of issue the amount of note-issues was equivalent to 4 % of deposits. There were 116 private banks of issue in England and Wales and the amount of notes was £2·6 m. If this was 5 % of deposits, then the deposits of the 116 banks would have been £52·0 m., or £450,000 per bank. At the same rate the deposits in the remaining 80 banks of non-issue would have been £36·0 m. Therefore, the total liabilities to the public of 196 banks would have been:

Note-issues of 116 banks	2·6 m.
Deposits of 116 banks	52·0 m.
Deposits of 80 banks	36·0 m.
Total	90·6 m.

(C) The 1875 Committee obtained answers from 143 provincial private banks and their total deposits were 60·7 m., or £420,000 per bank. At the same rate the deposits in the remaining 53 banks would have been £22·5 m. If we add 2·5 m. of note-issues to these, the total liabilities to the public of the 196 private banks would have been £85·7 m.

In conclusion, Dun put the amount of the total liabilities to the public of provincial private banks in England and Wales at £85·0 m.

Thus the liabilities to the public of provincial banks in England and Wales, both private and joint-stock, were estimated to be £219·0 m. in 1874. The paid-up capital of provincial joint-stock banks was £19·3 m. and their reserve fund was £9·2 m. The capital and reserve fund of provincial private banks cannot be estimated and Dun arbitrarily put them at £8·5 m. or 10 % of the liabilities to the public. Thus the total liabilities of the provincial banks were estimated to be £256·0 m. All the Scottish banks published their balance-sheets and their total liabilities were £105·9 m. The paid-up capital of Irish banks was £6·8 m., reserve fund £2·7 m., and note-issues £7·2 m. Only 5 of the 9 Irish banks of the time published their balance-sheets, but Dun obtained the figure of £31·7 m. as their total deposits from Dr Hancock,[1] so that the total liabilities were £48·4 m.

The next step was to ascertain the proportion of discounts to the total liabilities. Twenty-six provincial joint-stock banks had total liabilities of £55,445,000, and discounts and advances together amounted to £40,140,000 or 72·5 % of the total liabilities. But only 13 provincial banks disclosed the breakdown between discounted bills and advances. They had £9,630,000 of discounts against £9,845,000 of advances (both of these figures were partly estimated, as some banks did not distinguish between bills and cash, while others did not discriminate between advances and securities or money at call).

Furthermore, 8 provincial banks with discounts and advances of £20,458,000 showed in their accounts that their rebate on bills discounted amounted to £85,000. Dun thought that the average unlapsed currency of bills held by banks in 1874 was 49 days, as was quoted in the previous chapter.[2] Hence, applying the rate of interest of 5 %, he estimated that the amount of bills discounted of these 8 banks was £12,660,000, or 62 % of total loans and discounts. 'But these eight banks are all in commercial districts, where customers' bills are more abundant than in rural areas, and I venture to think that for the whole of provincial England the bills and advances may be taken to stand to one another in the very equal ratio of 50 to 50.'[3]

Thus, bills discounted were estimated to be 36·3 % of the total liabilities of English provincial banks. As has been mentioned, the latter amounted to £256·0 m., so that 36·3 % of the amount was £92·8 m.[4]

---

[1] Probably this refers to William Neilson Hancock, who wrote a number of books and pamphlets on the economic questions of Ireland during the third quarter of the nineteenth century.

    The amount of deposits by Irishmen for 1859–85 was later published by T. W. Grimshaw, Registrar-General of Ireland. See *The Economist*, 27 March 1886. The figure of £31·7 m. for 1874 given by Dr Hancock exactly agrees with the figure in *The Economist*, so that this is deposits by Irishmen only and is smaller than the total deposits of the nine Irish banks.

[2] Dun, 'The Banking Institutions', p. 87.

[3] *Ibid.*, p. 88.

[4] *Ibid.*, pp. 118–19.

The same procedure was followed in the cases of Scottish and Irish banks.

Among Scottish banks Clydesdale Banking Co. and British Linen Company showed their amounts of discounted bills, which together totalled £9,276,000, or 66 % of the total discounts and advances. Of the Irish banks, three, Hibernian, National and Royal, disclosed the amount of discounts, which was £7,368,000 in aggregate and was 67 % of the total discounts and advances. Therefore, Dun decided that 60 % of discounts and advances of Scottish and Irish banks belonged to the former category.

Bills and advances of Scottish banks were £76·2 m., so that discounts were estimated to be £45·7 m.[1]

Four Irish banks with total liabilities of £19,280,000 had bills and advances of £13,572,000 or 69 % of the total liabilities. As the total liabilities of all the Irish banks were £48·4 m., their discounts and advances were estimated at £33·4 m., of which discounts amounted to £20·0 m.[2]

According to Dun, therefore, the total amount of bills discounted by local banks (English provincial banks, Scottish banks and Irish banks) was £158·5 m. in 1874. We do not know what proportion of these was accounted for by inland bills. Clearly Liverpool banks must have had some foreign bills and some Scottish banks had London offices where they probably acquired foreign bills directly or through bill-brokers. Even so, the proportion of inland bills in the portfolios of local banks was most probably far higher than in the bill cases of London banks.

The next attempt was made by James Dick.[3]

By the time Dick made his estimate more joint-stock banks published balance-sheets. Of the 97 provincial joint-stock banks 80 published their balance-sheets. Of the 9 Irish banks 8 disclosed their figures. All the Scottish banks, of course, continued to publish their accounts.

The total bills and advances of the 80 provincial joint-stock banks in England and Wales amounted to £119,675,000. As 29 of these banks disclosed the amount of their discounted bills and these were equivalent to 36·6 % of the total bills and advances, the discounted bills of the 80 banks as a whole would have been £43,801,000. Dick also estimated the amount of bills discounted of the 17 remaining banks. He somehow estimated that their bills and advances were £6,000,000. (How he arrived at this figure is mysterious. I have made various but fruitless calculations to identify his method of estimation. Dick offers no explanation.) As 36·6 % of £6,000,000 is £2,196,000, he gave the figure of £45,997,000 as the amount of discounted bills held by these 97 banks.

[1] *Ibid.*   [2] *Ibid.*
[3] James Dick, 'Banking Statistics—A Record of Nine Years' Progress', *Journal of the Institute of Bankers*, 1884.

Dick similarly stated the proportion of bills to total discounts and advances in 6 Scottish banks to be 51·1 % and he applied this ratio to the total bills and advances of all the 10 Scottish banks of £67,615,000 to reach the figure of £34,554,000.

As for Irish banks, the bills and advances of 8 of them amounted to £26,379,000 and those of the one bank that did not publish a balance-sheet, the Bank of Ireland, were estimated to be £9,500,000 (again I do not know how). Three of the Irish banks published the amount of discounts and these were 58·4 % of total discounts and advances. The amount of discounted bills was, therefore, estimated to be £20,954,000.

Dick made no effort to estimate the amount of bills discounted by provincial private banks in England and Wales, but he estimated their deposits. As 72 provincial joint-stock banks with 1,021 offices had deposits of £135,858,000, the 175 private banks with 599 offices should have had £80 m. of deposits. As the deposits of the 80 provincial joint-stock banks (including note-issues) were £135,168,000 and their estimated amount of discounts was £44 m., the discounts of private banks might be thought to have been 32 % of the 80 m. + 1·6 m. (note-issues). This gives a figure of £20 m.

The aggregate amount of bills discounted by local banks in 1883 was, therefore, £122 m.

Thus, bills discounted by local banks declined from £158 m. in 1874 to £122 m. in 1883, or by 23 %. The amount of bills drawn decreased between these two dates from £1,631 m. to £1,334 m., or by 18 %. But the amount of inland bills outstanding was probably reduced by a considerably bigger percentage than this. The decline in the amount of bills discounted by local banks may, therefore, have been commensurate with or a little less than the reduction in the amount of inland bills outstanding at one time. As has been mentioned at the outset, however, both of these estimates are too tricky to be allowed to serve as a basis for further analysis. The results obtained do not refute (nor do they corroborate) the surmise that local banks may have come to hold a bigger share of inland bills outstanding, because they ceased to re-discount the bills they acquired.

Dick made another effort to ascertain the amount of bills discounted by banks in 1891.[1] His principle was the same as that for 1883. His results were as follows: 111 English provincial joint-stock banks, £35 m.; 10 Scottish banks, £28 m.; 9 Irish banks, £13 m. (He gave the figures to the order of thousands of pounds of sterling, but clearly such fine figures are meaningless, so that the figures under millions are omitted by rounding.) Thus local banks had £76 m. of bills in 1891. However, Dick made no estimate as to provincial private banks. We have,

[1] James Dick, 'Banks and Banking in the United Kingdom in 1891', *Journal of the Institute of Bankers*, 1892.

therefore, to compare this amount with that of bills discounted by local joint-stock banks in 1883, which was £102 m.

The amount of bills drawn in 1891 was £1,276 m., a decrease of 4 % from 1883. Therefore, the proportion of bills held by local joint-stock banks must have declined in the interval. This was largely due to the fact that many first-class provincial banks either went up to London to become London and provincial banks or were absorbed by these banks. Thus, according to Dick's estimate, 7 London and provincial banks had £30 m. of bills in 1883, but in 1891 17 London and provincial banks had £36 m. of them.

The fourth attempt was also made by Dick for 1896.[1] The method employed is the same as that used for 1891. The amount of bills discounted of the local banks was as follows: 88 English provincial joint-stock banks, £30 m.; 10 Scottish banks, £24 m.; 9 Irish banks, £15 m. Thus, the total amount of bills held by local joint-stock banks was £69 m. in that year.

In conclusion, King was quite right in pointing out that the supply of inland bills in the London discount market was very much affected by the discontinuance of the practice of re-discounting by banks in industrial counties. He seems to suggest that the cause of this development was the accumulation of savings deposits by these banks and the disrepute of the practice itself. The abuse of this system had repeatedly been made evident before the seventies, in 1825, 1836, 1847 and 1857. In view of the revival of the practice in every boom of the mid-nineteenth century, one may ask why re-discounting was not revived in the booms after the seventies. Evidently it was because inland bills themselves became scarce. On the other hand, there was probably accumulation of savings deposits in banks, as was suggested by King. During the Great Depression, bank deposits increased much more than discounts and advances, so that the proportion of the latter to the former experienced a conspicuous fall from the seventies to the nineties. The fall in this ratio was in itself a powerful factor in reducing the amount of bills, for the banks, in order to make up for the reduction in bills discounted, which was one cause of the decline of the ratio, strove to lend out their resources in the more illiquid form of overdrafts. They were able to do this precisely because the ratio became lower. In the mid-nineteenth century, when the ratio was very often far in excess of 100 %, banks had to rely on the London discount market for the supply of cash. Thus, overdrafts, which could not be converted into cash by re-discounting, were avoided as much as possible by country banks in industrial districts. After the seventies the ratio went down and there was no longer a need to re-discount, so that the reason to avoid over-

[1] James Dick, 'Banking Statistics of the United Kingdom in 1896 compared with former years', *Journal of the Institute of Bankers*, 1897.

drafts as a means of accommodating customers vanished. As customers were enabled to use the facility more liberally, they preferred it in order to make payment by cheques instead of bills. They could enjoy the rebate on cash payment, and the liability on overdrafts was in any case more flexible than that on bills. Thus, there was less occasion for the creation of bills.

In the next chapter this last point is discussed in more detail.

5. BANK OVERDRAFTS AND CASH PAYMENT

So far two causes of the reduction in the supply of inland bills in the London discount market have been discussed: the shortening of the average usance of inland bills and the discontinuance of the practice of re-discounting of bills by local banks. Although these changes were both powerful influences in diminishing the supply of inland bills in Lombard Street, they could not affect in themselves the amount of inland bills drawn, which began to decrease after 1873.

It is often said that the liability on bills accepted is inelastic, in that the payment has to be effected at the due date under any circumstances, whereas the liability in the form of overdrawn accounts with banks is flexible, because repayment can be postponed or accelerated at the debtors' convenience. It is sometimes inferred from this that firms in modern times have come to prize this flexibility of overdraft facilities and have come to prefer borrowing from the banks in this form to accepting bills drawn upon them, so that the creation of bills has become limited. Moreover, firms can get a rebate on cash payment if they overdraw their bank accounts and pay by cheque; the high cost of borrowing by overdraft compared with bill finance is offset thereby. It is often said that it was for this reason that bills became obsolete.

For example, in explaining the decline in the use of bills in international trade after the First World War, Balogh writes 'The very advantage of the bill from the point of view of the creditor seems to be the basic reason for the gradual shrinkage of the bill as a medium of finance. The fear of being faced with the necessity of paying a given amount of money at a certain date, however inconvenient for the debtor, must have prejudiced borrowers against the use of credits in the shape of bills, however cheap.'[1]

Such an argument is sometimes put forward also to explain the decline of inland bills in the seventies and the eighties. Thus, King writes, 'From many points of view, it became a matter of indifference to the banks whether they financed their customers by discounting their bills or by granting loans or advances, and to the customer the flexibility of the overdraft system had definite attractions.'[2]

It is evident that financiers would always have preferred the discounting of bills of exchange, and that debtors would have preferred a more elastic method of borrowing. If this was so, the choice of the

[1] T. Balogh, *Studies in Financial Organisation*, Cambridge, 1950, p. 180.
[2] King, *History of the London Discount Market*, p. 273.

method or form of lending must have depended upon the relative strength of the lenders and the borrowers at the time. Of course, this relative strength would have been largely determined by the slackness or tightness of the financial market. If bills were the predominant means of finance before the seventies and if they were subsequently superseded by overdrafts (which enabled cash payment to become prevalent), there must have been a decided change in the relative strengths of, and therefore in the relationship between, the supply of and the demand for money. Clearly, the plethora of money during the Great Depression had a strong influence in this respect.

As has been shown in the previous chapter, before the seventies banks in industrial counties had habitually to depend upon the London money market in accommodating their customers. This, of course, means that there was a strong demand for money from the customers and that the local banks were unable to satisfy the demand. Under such circumstances banks were unable or unwilling to grant overdrafts to their customers on a large scale. The reason for this was clearly explained in Thomas Bullion's 'Letters to a Branch Manager' in *Bankers' Magazine* of 1848:

And first, as respects the very common plea founded upon the safety of the overdraft. Undoubtedly one of the main considerations with a banker when he makes an advance is the certainty of its repayment....But with a banker there is a consideration beyond and above this. The safety of any particular account is one thing, the safety of his bank is quite another; ...An ordinary drain upon a bank whose business was chiefly confined to the discount of legitimate business bills, could be met by simply contracting the volume of its discounts; but you do not necessarily diminish your existing overdrafts a single pound by refusing to grant fresh ones, or, if the drain were too sudden and heavy to be met by a mere contraction of the discounts of the bank, a portion of its bills on hand might be converted into cash. In the worst of times (October last only excepted) good bills could be re-discounted at a price.[1]

Thus, if overdraft and cash payment were convenient to the bank's customers,[2] bills of exchange were convenient for the banks, because bills were unique in having the dual character of being at the same time the means of accommodating banks' customers and of being liquid assets for banks.

The liquidity of bills as banks' assets derived, of course, from their being re-discountable in London. If, for some reason or other, banks came to have no more need to re-discount bills in London, such liquidity

---

[1] *Bankers' Magazine*, 1848, pp. 470–1. Thomas Bullion was the pseudonym of George Rae, later chairman of the North and South Wales Bank, and these letters published in *Bankers' Magazine* were the first version of his famous book, *The Country Banker*. On this point, see 'Details in Country Banking' in *Bankers' Magazine*, July 1885.

[2] The banks' customers may act both in the capacity of sellers and buyers, but cash payment is convenient and favourable to the customers in either capacity. As buyers they can get the rebate on cash payment (and their liability on overdrawn accounts is more elastic than that on accepted bills) and as sellers they can avoid incurring the contingent liability on the bills drawn and also avoid the trouble and sometimes the cost of discounting the bills.

of bills would become largely valueless to them. Or, what comes to the same thing, if banks came to hold more liquid assets other than bills, such as money at call and short notice, they would become less selective in the forms of lending. For such a thing to happen, either the demand for money of customers has to decline or banks have to accumulate more longer-term deposits. In either case, such a change would be reflected in the lowering of the banks' advances plus discounts/deposits ratio, which will reflect the relationship between the supply of and the demand for money.

As has already been shown in the last chapter, banks in Liverpool in the middle of the nineteenth century were in an extremely overlent position: the ratio of advances plus discounts/deposits of these banks was normally in excess of 100 %. For example, for 31 December 1865 the ratio of the Liverpool Commercial Banking Co. was 159 %, and that of Liverpool Union Bank was 118 %. If we take into consideration the amount of re-discounted bills, we can indicate the extent to which the demand for money exceeded the supply.[1]

In such conditions it is natural that banks were unable to hold sufficient liquid assets other than bills to meet a contingency. The lowering of this ratio would have been the pre-condition for banks to be able to grant overdraft facilities to customers. Was such a state of things common to banks in other industrial counties and did the ratio go down after 1873 when the overdraft gradually became the standard form of bank lending?

The best material to test this point can be found in *Miscellaneous Statistics of the U.K.* of 1882,[2] where there is a table showing the paid-up capital, reserve fund, liabilities to the public other than note-issues, advances and discounts, investments in securities and other assets of joint-stock banks in the U.K. for 1870–80. In 1880 the total paid-up capital of all the joint-stock banks in England and Wales (including Bank of England, Anglo-Colonial and Anglo-Foreign banks with head offices in London) was £53 m. and banks with the aggregate paid-up capital of £49 m. co-operated with the authorities in the compilation of the statistics by disclosing their figures for the above-mentioned items of their balance-sheets.

From this we can calculate the advances plus discounts/deposits ratios of joint-stock banks for 1870–80. Since the figures by districts are given, we can see the change over time of this ratio for banks in each industrial district. However, the liabilities to the public in these statistics include acceptances, drafts on other banks, circular notes and so on. Drafts,

---

[1] 'Hence, the practice of the Liverpool and Manchester bankers consists more of indorsing and rendering valid, or approved, the bills created, and received, for the manufacturers of the district, than in receiving and disbursing of cash deposits;...' (J. Macardy, *Outline of Banks, Banking and Currency on the Basis of Manchester*, Manchester, 1842).

[2] BPP 1882, Vol. 74, pp. 622–7.

circular notes and other miscellaneous liabilities evidently cannot be more than a small fraction of the total liabilities, but acceptances were often very important with banks in London and cotton districts. We have, therefore, to deduct acceptances from the liabilities to the public and from advances and discounts in order to arrive at correct ratios. Unfortunately, exact amounts of acceptances were not stated. Most country banks seem to have lumped them together with other items in their balance-sheets, such as current and deposit accounts. This may have been done because of the minimal importance of acceptance business for ordinary country banks. On the other hand, banks in London and Liverpool, with the exception of the London Joint Stock Bank and the Bank of Liverpool, published balance-sheets stating the amounts of acceptances. The published amounts of acceptances of these banks were aggregated and deducted from the liabilities to the public and advances and discounts in *Miscellaneous Statistics*, and then the balance of the former was regarded as roughly equivalent to deposits and the ratios were calculated. As has been stated above, London Joint Stock Bank did not disclose the amount of acceptances until 1879, when it was £2,468,000 (at the end of the year). At this time the aggregate amount of acceptances of nine London banks which continuously published them for 1870–80, was £11,458,000. Therefore, the amount of acceptances shown in Table 23 for London banks is an undervaluation of about 20 %.

Although London Joint Stock Bank began to state its acceptances from 1879, its figures are not included in the aggregate acceptances of London banks, for the inclusion of the figures in the middle of the period would impair the basis for comparison of the yearly changes of the ratio. The same is true of the acceptances of cotton district banks. Only the acceptances of those banks publishing the figures throughout the period are taken; the amount of these acceptances was deducted both from the liabilities to the public and from advances and discounts of *Miscellaneous Statistics*. In this case, the Bank of Liverpool (later Martins Bank) and banks in Manchester including Manchester and Liverpool District Banking Co., and Manchester and Salford Bank (later Williams Deacon's Bank) did not publish their acceptances at the beginning of the period. Consequently, the figures of only five banks are taken, namely those of Liverpool Union, National Bank of Liverpool, North-Western, Parr's and Union Bank of Manchester. Their aggregate acceptances represent probably about one-third of the total for all the banks in cotton districts, for in 1880 the aggregate acceptances of these five banks amounted to £901,000, while those of the Bank of Liverpool were £891,000, those of Manchester and County £531,000, and those of Manchester and Liverpool District £42,000.

Of the banks in woollen and worsted districts only one bank, Bank of

Leeds, published these figures. Of the banks in other districts, North
and South Wales Bank (the head office of which was in Liverpool, but
which apparently *Miscellaneous Statistics* did not treat as a cotton district
bank) seems to be the only one publishing the amount of acceptances
throughout the period. As their acceptances amounted to a relatively
large sum, they should be deducted both from the liabilities to the
public and from advances and discounts in *Miscellaneous Statistics*.

The acceptances of individual banks and the aggregate amounts are
shown in Table 23. Table 24 shows the liabilities to the public, acceptances, advances and discounts and the ratio of advances plus discounts/
deposits of English and Welsh joint-stock banks (excluding the Bank of
England, Anglo-Colonial and Anglo-Foreign banks). From Table 24
we can see that the ratio for joint-stock banks in cotton districts was
104·6 % in 1870 and that it was 90·2 % in 1880. Similarly, the ratio for
woollen and worsted districts came down from 113·7 to 124·0 % in the
same period, while for the Midland banks it went down from 106·6 to
92·2 %. Thus, there is a broad parallelism in the movement of the ratio
for different industrial districts. We should note also that the downward
tendency of the ratio is common to other districts. The ratio for
Northumberland, Durham, Lancashire and Yorkshire (excluding cotton
and woollen and worsted districts) went down from 103·5 to 88·2 %.
This is a largely industrial district, which includes Newcastle-upon-
Tyne and Sheffield. (Of course, Northumberland, Durham and the
North and East Ridings of Yorkshire include large agricultural areas,
but as far as banking is concerned, the statistics would be dominated by
banks in the two industrial districts named above.) The ratio for
Gloucestershire, Monmouth and South Wales was 98·3 % in 1870 and
94·4 % in 1880. That for other English and Welsh counties (which were
largely 'agricultural') came down from 76·6 % to 71·4 %. Even for
London the trend was downward and the ratio fell from 78·6 to 70·6 %.

However, ten years would be too short a period to confirm a long-term
trend such as is the problem here. The high value of the ratio for 1870
may have been just an accidental aberration. Similarly, the downward
trend of the ratio may have been reversed in the next decade. Actually
there was such a reversal in 1878 when the collapse of City of Glasgow
Bank and of the West of England and South Wales District Bank
occasioned runs on banks and there was a general decrease of bank
deposits, which caused the ratio to go up considerably.

Therefore, we should supplement *Miscellaneous Statistics* with figures
from other sources which cover a longer period of time. The only source
for such supplementary statistics is the published balance-sheets of
banks. Unfortunately, as is well known, these published balance-sheets
are defective in a number of ways. The earlier they are, the more
defective they are. To give an extreme example, Sheffield and Hallam-

shire Bank before 1870 gave only two items on the asset side, which were 'cash in the bank, bills discounted, balances owing by customers, and other securities' and 'bank premise and furniture'. Many banks did not distinguish between advances and investment in securities, while some banks, mostly in Yorkshire, lumped together cash and bills discounted in the same item.

In order to calculate the ratio in question, we have, therefore, to choose only those balance-sheets which at least distinguished between deposits, acceptances, and capital accounts on the liability side and differentiated advances and discounts from cash in hand and at call, securities and bank premises. There were only twenty-three banks before 1870 which made such distinctions in their balance-sheets. Even then, there are numerous ambiguities. First, such items as drafts current, credits issued, bills for collection and other miscellaneous liabilities were in many cases classed with deposit and current accounts. However, these are minor items and their inclusion or exclusion is not likely to distort the ratio substantially. Secondly, many banks discriminated between British Government securities and other securities and the latter were often included in advances. It is unlikely, however, that such 'other securities' amounted to much in most cases. Moreover, 'other securities' sometimes encompassed more than investment securities, for instance promissory notes of borrowers and other bank advances on security. For example, London and Yorkshire Bank's balance-sheets had the following two items, 'securities, consisting of Consols, India and Colonial Government and other investments' and 'bills discounted, advances and other securities'. Thirdly, some, or rather, most country banks and a few London banks included a part of their money at short notice in advances. In particular, money lent to the Stock Exchange at a fortnight's notice was in most instances lumped together with ordinary advances. As banks in industrial areas tended to increase the amount of money employed in London after the eighties, the inclusion of money at short notice in advances would make for an overestimate of the ratio. Fourthly, the treatment of Treasury Bills, County Council Bills and so on seems to differ from bank to bank. For instance, the London and Provincial Bank included Treasury Bills in advances and discounts in its balance-sheets of 31 December 1890, while Birmingham Banking Co. included them in investments in its balance-sheet of 30 June 1879. Fifthly, when a bank did not make any mention of a particular item in the balance-sheet, we cannot know whether it was tacitly included in some other item or if in fact it existed at all. For example, if there was no reference to investment in securities, we cannot know whether the bank did not hold any investment securities (which is quite possible with banks in industrial districts which were in an overlent position) or if the securities were included in advances. In such a case, it was presumed that, if the title of the item was simply 'advances and discounts', it did not include securities, but that, if the title was 'advances, discounts, &c.', it did contain securities. Balance-sheets of the latter category (namely those which lacked an item for securities and had an item entitled in the above way) were not utilized in the calculation of the ratio.

In spite of these ambiguities we have to rely on the published balance-sheets of banks in order to see the movement of the ratio before 1870 and after 1880. Probably we might expect the movement of the ratios to reflect that of the true advances plus discounts/deposits ratios, even if the absolute values of the ratios calculated from published balance-sheets differ somewhat from the true values. Table 25 gives the ratio of twenty-three joint-stock banks of the several districts of England and Wales for 1865–70. The aggregate deposits of these twenty-three banks in 1870 were £61,089,000. As the total liabilities to the public of English and Welsh joint-stock banks (excluding Bank of England and Anglo-Colonial and Anglo-Foreign banks) according to *Miscellaneous Statistics* were £169,035,000 in 1870, the figures obtained from these twenty-three banks represent about one-third of the total joint-stock banks statistics.

Table 26 gives the ratio of forty-six joint-stock banks for 1880–96. (Of course, the number of banks decreases in later years because of bank amalgamations, forty-six being the number in 1881.) The aggregate deposits of these forty-six banks were £196,340,000 in 1881 (for 1880 figures for Manchester and Salford Bank cannot be obtained, so that the aggregate deposits for 1880 of £179,317,000 are for forty-five banks only). According to *Miscellaneous Statistics* the total liabilities to the public of English and Welsh joint-stock banks were £245,544,000 in 1880, so that the figures obtained from the forty-six banks represent nearly two-thirds of all the joint-stock banks in England and Wales.

From Tables 25 and 26 we can see that the ratios were normally in excess of 100 % for banks in industrial districts before 1870 and that they never exceeded 100 % after 1880 in any districts, if we except banks in woollen and worsted areas, although a strict comparison is impossible because the figures were obtained from different banks for pre-1870 years and post-1880 years. Even for banks in woollen and worsted districts the ratios after 1880 were definitely lower than those for pre-1870 period.

Thus, the downward tendency of the ratio observed in Table 24 can be confirmed. This tendency continued after 1880 and by 1896 the difference of the ratios from district to district was much smaller than in 1870. In 1870 the ratio ranged from 133·7 % for woollen and worsted districts to 76·6 % for 'other English and Welsh counties' (largely agricultural), but in 1896 the highest ratio was 80·0 % for woollen and worsted districts and the lowest was 57·7 % for other English and Welsh counties. We must note that the ratio came down not only in industrial areas but also in 'agricultural' counties.

After 1896, because of bank amalgamations, it becomes meaningless to take the ratios by districts. Therefore, only the ratio for the whole of England and Wales will be considered. Although most joint-stock banks and some private banks had begun to publish balance-sheets by this time, only the figures for banks in Table 26 are taken in the calculation of the ratio. This is in order not to impair the basis for comparison of the ratio before and after 1896. From Table 27 it will be seen that the ratio remained at about the same level of 60–66 % for the years 1897–1913. The ratio for the whole of England and Wales in 1870 was 88·2 %, as is seen from Table 24. There was, therefore, a considerable decline in the ratio from the seventies to the nineties.

What, then, was the cause of this decline? Evidently, it must have been due to the increase in deposits, or to the decrease in advances and discounts, or to a combination of both. From Table 24 it appears that the chief cause was the increase in deposits. For example, in the cotton districts the bank deposits increased from £15,445,000 in 1870 to £26,516,000 in 1880 or by 72 %, while advances and discounts grew from £16,152,000 to £23,926,000 or by only 48 %. In the woollen and worsted districts the growth of deposits was by 70 % from £6,753,000 to £11,424,000 and that of advances and discounts was by 57 % from £9,027,000 to £14,171,000. In the Midlands, including Birmingham, deposits increased from £10,004,000 to £17,760,000 or by 78 %, while advances and discounts increased from £10,666,000 to £16,370,000 or by 53 %.

The tendency for deposits to increase more rapidly than advances and discounts continued after 1880, as will be seen from Table 26.

Clearly this large increase in deposits is associated with the increase in bank offices discussed in Chapter 1. However, we must note that even with banks which did not indulge in branch extension the ratio went down. For instance, Liverpool Commercial Banking Co. remained a unit bank until it was absorbed by the Bank of Liverpool in 1888. The ratio of advances plus discounts/deposits of this bank was as high as 159 % for 31 December 1865, but in 1887 just before its amalgamation with the Bank of Liverpool the ratio was down to 118 %. The same is true of Liverpool Union Bank, which had only one office until 1878 and only three even in 1891. The ratio for this bank was 118 % for 31 December 1865, 102 % in 1878 and 101 % in 1887.

In these two cases, too, the chief cause of the decline in the ratio was the increase in deposits. The average deposits of Liverpool Commercial Banking Co. for 1865–9 were £733,000 and the average for 1883–7 was £921,000, while the average advances and discounts were £1,004,000 for 1865–9 and £1,091,000 for 1883–7. The average deposits of this bank grew by 26 % and the average advances and discount by only 8 %. If we take into account the amount of re-discounted bills, it may be safely said that the lending business of the bank experienced a positive decline. Furthermore, it must be noted that the average discounts of the bank were £629,000 in 1865–9 and £534,000 in 1883–7, so that there was an absolute decrease in the discounts. On the other hand, loans and advances increased from the average of £375,000 to £557,000 during the same period. In spite of the increase in deposits, therefore, there were fewer bills to discount and the bank maintained the level of its lending by increasing loans and advances.

The same thing is true of Liverpool Union Bank. The average deposits grew from £1,610,000 in 1865–9 to £2,415,000 in 1883–7 or by 50 %, while the average advances and discounts grew from £1,862,000 to £2,497,000 or by 34 %. In this case, too, the average discounts experienced an absolute decline from £1,625,000 to £1,359,000.

Thus there seems to have been a considerable change in the relationship between the supply of money and the demand for it in the industrial counties of England and Wales during the Great Depression. Before 1873 an extremely high level of the ratio of advances plus discounts/deposits was the rule for all the industrial districts, showing that there was a strong demand for money in these areas, which the local banks could not satisfy without relying upon the money market in London. As has been suggested at the beginning of this chapter, the banks had to accommodate the customers in the most liquid form possible under these circumstances, for they were lent up to the hilt and could not afford to hold enough liquid assets. Thus, bills of exchange, which served both as the means of lending to the customers and as liquid assets, were invaluable to the banks. It may also be said that the financial market was a lenders' market and banks could largely disregard the convenience of the borrowers.

With the fall of the ratio of advances plus discounts/deposits after 1873 the relationship between the lender and the borrower must have experienced a marked change. For one thing banks could now hold more liquid assets other than bills and had no more reason to cling to the discount of bills as the form of lending. For another, in order to maintain the level of profit they now had to comply with the wishes of the customers and grant the facility of overdraft. As has been mentioned, if overdrafts became prevalent, there would be less occasion for the creation of bills. To a certain extent, this is a circular argument implying that the decrease of bills caused banks to expand advances, which reduced bills still more. However, in association with other structural changes, such as the increase in longer-term deposits and the shortening of the average usance of inland bills, the prevalence of overdrafts will go a long way towards explaining the decline in the amount of bills drawn.

Contemporary verbal evidence is almost unanimous in ascribing the cause of the reduction in the amount of bills to the spread of cash payment, which undoubtedly was made possible by overdrafts. Unfortunately, this verbal evidence is no substitute for a detailed study of the phenomenon and it would be useless to quote many of them. A typical example is found in an article in *The Economist* of 6 October 1883, which is entitled 'The Number and Amount of Bills in Circulation'. It is stated there that 'For the decrease in the number of bills good reasons can be assigned. They have, to some extent, been supplanted by telegraphic transfers, and of late, also, cash payments have obtained much more largely than formerly, traders preferring to pay by means of advances from their bankers rather than by bills.'[1]

---

[1] Similar evidence on the spread of cash payments can be found in numerous places: *The Economist*, 25 August 1877, p. 1006 ('Business Notes—The Supply of Bills in the Discount Market'); 24 August 1878, p. 1001 ('The Fortnightly Review on Banking'); 29 May 1880, p. 613 ('The Money Market'); 24 October 1885, p. 1292 ('Some Points in a Review of Banking during the Last Year'); *The Statist*, 1880, p. 487 ('The Last Banking Half Year'); *The Bankers' Magazine*, 1883, p. 252, pp. 254–5 ('Speech at Bank Meetings'); 1896, pp. 374–5 ('Bills of Exchanges held by Bankers').

There are also references to the tendency to cash payment in the Royal Commission on Depression of Trade and Industry, *Minutes of Evidence*, BPP 1886, Vol. 21, QQ. 388, 577, 583 and 888.

6. SOME CONSEQUENCES OF THE DECLINE OF INLAND BILLS

I CORRELATION OF THE AMOUNTS OF BILLS AND THE DISCOUNT RATES

We have seen that the amount of bills supplied to the London money market declined for a number of reasons: the average usance of inland bills became shorter; banks accumulated more longer-term deposits, as the number of bank offices increased and the banking habit spread among the general public, so that the ratio of advances plus discounts/deposits declined markedly in the industrial counties, with the result that banks came to hold the bills to maturity and discontinued the practice of re-discounting them in London; there was a general preference for cash payment, the spread of which was made possible by the changed attitude of banks in regard to overdrafts. The operation of these forces would not have been limited to domestic finance only: they must also have affected the financing of international trade. Banks (including those in countries other than the United Kingdom) with their increased liquidity would have become better able to grant overdraft facilities to their customers who wanted to pay for their imports by cheques, or, what comes to the same thing, by telegraphic transfers, as soon as the import contracts were made.

That such forces were at work in regard to foreign trade seems to be attested by the fact that the amount of foreign bills drawn came to represent a smaller and smaller ratio of the foreign trade of the U.K. after the seventies.

The annual average of foreign bills drawn during the five years 1866–70 was £595 m., while the average value of foreign trade (imports plus exports plus re-exports) was £528 m. Foreign bills were, therefore, equivalent to 113 % of foreign trade. In the trough of the Great Depression of 1893–7, foreign bills amounted to £665 m. on the average and foreign trade to £710 m., so that the former was 94 % of the latter. In the five-year period 1909–13, the average amount of foreign bills was £1,050 m. and of foreign trade £1,258 m., so that the ratio now declined to 84 %.

Thus, in spite of the large increase in the amount of foreign bills, their proportion to foreign trade actually fell considerably. Furthermore, a large proportion of foreign bills at the later dates was drawn for the finance of trade between third countries and, as will be shown later, another large portion consisted of finance bills drawn to take advantage of international interest rate differences. We are entitled to say, therefore, that bills were used less and less in the finance and settlement of British foreign trade.

Even so, the absolute amount of foreign bills increased conspicuously after 1894. In addition, the amount of inland bills ceased to decrease after that year and showed a slight tendency to increase towards the end of the period now in question. This requires explanation. Part of the explanation can doubtless be found in the growth of the acceptance business of London. To foreigners financing of trade by bills on London must have been cheaper than cash payment, which involved borrowing from their local banks.

Part of the explanation, however, seems to lie in the changed nature of bills. Before the Committee on Finance and Industry (Macmillan Committee) 1931, Sir Robert Kindersley gave the following evidence,

> ...I think one can say this, that a low discount rate, provided you do not have finance bills, does not stimulate the amount of drawing. I have been trying to get a figure of pre-War acceptances *apropos* of this and I am told of bills in 1913, prime acceptances, was £350,000,000, and of that £350,000,000 60 per cent were finance bills. It was a figure that astonished me, but it came from a source that I believe to be reliable.[1]

As the total amount of bills drawn in 1913 was £1,854 m. and, assuming that the average usance was three months, the amount of bills outstanding at one time in that year would have been £450,000,000, the figure given by Kindersley of £350,000,000 of prime acceptances seems to be quite reasonable. If 60 % of this were finance bills, it would seem that the vigorous increase in bills after 1894 was principally due to the growth in the amount of finance bills.

As Kindersley's evidence is not in the nature of a serious study of the subject, we must endeavour to ascertain whether it is true or not that the larger part of bills in pre-1913 years was finance bills.

As is evident, the volume of finance bills drawn on London must have been sensitive to short-term rates of interest in London, while bills for the finance of trade would increase and decrease with the volume of trade.[2] More precisely, the amount of bills for the finance of trade would

---

[1] Committee on Finance and Industry, 1931, *Minutes of Evidence*, Q. 1273.

[2] 'On the assets side, for example, one would have to draw a distinction between acceptances representing commercial bills and finance bills, respectively. The former, it is generally believed, do not appear to have been much affected by higher short-term interest rates in London. Foreign importers in the pre-1914 world were not able easily to shift acceptance financing to other centres, simply because the necessary facilities outside of London were generally quite limited. Besides, foreign commercial borrowers were in any case probably reluctant to alter long-standing credit lines or banking connections in London because of temporary rate increases and to shop around for alternative sources of credit elsewhere. It is not unlikely, moreover, that a rise in the discount rate as such would have made London accepting houses, whose main concern was the ratio of their acceptance liabilities to their capital, less willing to enter into acceptance commitment on behalf of credit-worthy foreign customers. London discount houses, however, at a time of monetary stringency, might have been somewhat more reluctant to take up bills that were offered or

increase in a boom, and this would cause the rate of discount to rise, since the supply of bills (= demand for money) is increased. The volume of finance bills, on the other hand, would decrease when the London rate of discount was high. Thus the behaviour of the two kinds of bills would be radically different in regard to interest rates, finance bills having a negative correlation with the discount rate and commercial bills having a positive correlation with it. We may, therefore, gauge what was the proportion of finance bills in the total supply by taking the correlation of the amount of bills drawn with the discount rate. If finance bills were dominant in the total supply of bills, it would tend to have negative correlation with the rate of discount.

The amount of bills drawn has been estimated in Chapter 2. As these amounts are for financial years, it would be better to use the average discount rates for financial years. (It should be noted that, if there were time lags between the drawing of bills and the movement of the discount rate, they would be in the reverse directions for finance bills and commercial bills. The volume of finance bills would lag behind the change in the discount rate, while changes in the amounts of commercial bills would precede those of the discount rate. It would not be desirable, therefore, to correlate the average discount rates for calendar years with the amounts of bills for financial years.)

Surprisingly enough, nobody has yet calculated the monthly average rates of discount for the pre-1913 years. Even the yearly averages were calculated in a very unsatisfactory manner. T. T. Williams calculated the averages for calendar years of the market rate of discount of three months' bank bills in London for 1845–1910.[1] E. G. Peake gave the yearly average discount rates of three months' bank bills and six months' bank bills for 1882–1913.[2] These, however, were simply the averages of the twelve quotations on the first Thursdays of the twelve months of the calendar year. This gap in the historical statistics, however, has recently been partly made good by S. Homer, *A History of Interest Rates*,[3] which gives the yearly average rate of discount of three months' bank bills from 1800. Unfortunately, Homer's figures are for calendar years. I have, therefore, calculated the monthly average discount rates from

have been more selective in their purchases. On the other hand, foreign drawings of finance bills on London houses appear to have been quite sensitive to higher short-term interest rates, since these borrowings were motivated primarily by relative interest rates in London and abroad. To the extent that a rise in the Bank rate had the effect of reducing Britain's foreign acceptance claims, it was mainly on this component, which may have represented more than half of the outstanding total in 1913, that it must have acted.'
A. I. Bloomfield, *Short-Term Capital Movements under the Pre-1914 Gold Standard*, Princeton, 1963, pp. 75–6.

[1] T. T. Williams, 'The Rate of Discount and the Price of Consols', *Journal of the Royal Statistical Society*, 1912.
[2] E. G. Peake, *An Academic Study of Some Money Market and Other Statistics*, London, 1923.
[3] S. Homer, *A History of Interest Rates*, New Brunswick, New Jersey, 1963.

the weekly quotations given in *The Economist*.[1] The monthly averages for
April to March (i.e. the financial year) have then been again averaged
to obtain yearly averages. The following rates have been taken from
The Economist to calculate monthly and yearly averages: day-to-day
money rate, market rate of discount of three months' bank bills, market
rate of discount of six months' bank bills, Bank rate, Paris market rate
of discount, New York call money rate and Berlin market rate of
discount. The monthly averages of these rates for 1855–1913 are shown
in Table 30. The yearly averages of market rates of discount of three
months' bank bills are shown in Table 28. Although these yearly
averages are not the true ones in that they are not the averages of all the
working days of the years, they are still the averages of 52 Thursdays of
the years.

The market rates of discount for three months' bank bills in Table 28
are then correlated with the amounts of bills drawn. The correlations
are for deviations from the linear trends throughout unless otherwise
mentioned. They are calculated for three periods: 1855–70, 1871–92,
and 1893–1913. The selection of these dates was largely necessitated by
the circumstance that the Inland Revenue Office published the breakdown between revenue from stamps on inland bills and that from
foreign bills for the two periods of 1855–70 and 1893–1913; during the
intermediate years of 1871–92 it did not publish this information. By
coincidence these dates broadly agree with the turning points of the
'Kondratieff cycle', which the alternating trends in the amounts of
bills drawn closely follow, so that the selection of the periods would be
on the whole appropriate for removal of the trends.

The results are as follows:

Period	1855–70	1871–92	1893–1913
Inland bills and discount rates	+0·91	—	+0·21
Foreign bills and discount rates	+0·91	—	+0·09
Total bills and discount rates	+0·91	+0·71	+0·12

Thus there was a strong positive correlation between the amounts of
bills drawn and discount rates in the middle of the nineteenth century,
suggesting that the bills were mainly commercial bills which naturally
increased in a boom when interest rates were high and decreased in a
depression when they were low. On the other hand, for 1893–1913 the
behaviour of the amounts of bills with respect to discount rates was
radically different from that of the mid-nineteenth century. Although
the correlation is not actually negative, the coefficients are almost equal
to zero in the case of foreign bills. Even the inland bills do not have any

[1] *The Economist* was published each Friday, so that the rates published there were those
current on Thursday of each week.

meaningful correlation with discount rates. This suggests, of course, that there was a large admixture of finance bills which tended to increase when discount rates were low and *vice versa*.

There may, however, be an objection that the drawing of finance bills was chiefly conditioned by interest rate differentials between London and foreign centres, and not by the absolute levels of London rates. These differentials were, therefore, calculated from the monthly figures shown in Table 30 and are given in Table 29. They are, of course, averaged for financial years in the same way as the London market rate of discount of three months' bank bills in Table 28. *The Economist*, however, did not give foreign rates of interest before 1860. For 1861–80 the only leading overseas rate it published was that for Paris. This may appear unsatisfactory, but in those early years New York was an isolated market and Berlin was not an important financial market before the Franco–Prussian War. Thus the discount rate differentials between London and Paris were calculated for 1861–1913 (by subtracting the Paris rate from the London rate, so that, when the London rate was lower than the Paris rate, the differential would carry a minus sign)[1] and correlated with the amounts of bills. (It is presumed that interest rate differentials have no trends.)[2]

The results are as follows:

Period	1861–70	1871–80	1881–92	1893–1913
Inland bills and differentials	+0·62	—	—	−0·15
Foreign bills and differentials	+0·57	—	—	−0·27
Total bills and differentials	+0·60	+0·26	+0·42	−0·26

For 1881–1913 the averages of the Paris market rate, the New York call money rate and the Berlin market rate have been calculated and the differentials between the London market rates and these averages (calculated by subtracting the averages of foreign rates from London rates) are correlated with the amounts of bills. (The averages of foreign rates, and the differentials between London and average foreign rates, are shown in Table 29.)

The results are as follows:

Period	1881–92	1893–1913
Inland bills and differentials	—	−0·18
Foreign bills and differentials	—	−0·32
Total bills and differentials	+0·26	−0·29

[1] The reason for calculating the differential in this way is that the London discount rate and the differentials would move in the same direction: i.e. when the London rate was low the differential would tend to have minus sign.

[2] The secular trends of interest rates in different countries in this period were more or less in the same direction: downwards in 1873–94 and upwards in 1894–1913. Thus differentials would have no conspicuous trends.

The fairly strong positive correlation between the bills and the London–Paris discount rate differentials for 1861–70 is in fact meaningless. This is because London rates fluctuated much more than Paris rates which were famous for their stability. As bills had strong positive correlation with the London discount rates, and the London–Paris differentials reflected on the whole the movement of the London rates, there occurred a spurious positive correlation between bills and the differentials. If it means anything, it is that the amount of bills was not sensitive to international interest rate differences.

On the other hand, the negative values of the correlation coefficients for the 1893–1913 period may be thought to be more meaningful than their absolute values seem to suggest. There are two reasons for thinking this. One is that, even though the amount of finance bills appears to have increased consistently after the seventies, they appear never to have constituted the overwhelming bulk of the total volume of bills. If one part of the bills consisted of commercial bills having a positive correlation with interest rates and another part of finance bills having a negative correlation with them, the overall behaviour of the total amount of bills, whether inland or foreign, would tend to be neutral to the movement of interest rates.

The second reason is that, if we exclude the period 1906–13, the negative correlation between bills and discount rates after the nineties becomes much more pronounced. After 1906 the correlation is on the whole positive. The boom of 1906–7, its collapse in 1907, the ensuing depression of 1908–9, and the growing political tension with international armament competition after 1910 had a profound effect on money markets. The vigorous boom of 1906–7 seems to have prompted speculators in other countries, especially the United States, to draw bills on London and to obtain money there, in spite of the fact that the interest rates were higher in London. In the depression of 1908–9 the reverse seems to have happened. Although London money rates were lower than elsewhere, bills were not drawn on London, and the British were chary of lending money abroad.[1] Moreover, the amount of foreign

---

[1] This is pointed out by Neisser. 'Im übrigen dürfen wir die Entwicklung der Abstandkurse [disparity between the movements of London–Berlin discount rate differentials and the course of exchange of pound sterling in marks] seit 1907 als einem weiteren Beweis für die schon mehrfach aufgestellte Behauptung ersehen, dass nach 1907 das Konjunkturbewusstsein der grossen Geldgeber und ihr Gefül für Verantwortlichkeit gewachsen ist. Nach den Erfahrungen von 1907 trat eine erhebliche Zurückerhaltung des englischen Geldkapitals im Auslandesgeschäft ein. Auch in der Depression entschloss man sich von da an schwerer, Kapitalien in das höhere Zinsen zahlende Deutschland zu legen, eine Zurückerhaltung, die natürlich zu einer relativen Erhöhung des Niveaus des Pfundkurses über das Niveau der Diskontdifferenzlinie führen musste.' ('Besides we may regard the development of the disparity curve since 1907 as a further proof for the assertion which has already been made several times, that after 1907 the awareness of great financiers of economic fluctuations and their sense of responsibility have grown. After the experiences of 1907 a marked withholding of English money from foreign business became apparent.

bills drawn would be influenced not only by short-term interest rate differentials, but also by the amount of new issues of long-term securities in London, which increased markedly after 1910. Thus, although discount rates were higher in London after 1910 than in other markets, the volume of bills increased greatly, showing a strong positive correlation with interest rates.

Another point worth noting is that even inland bills came to have a slightly negative correlation with international interest rate differentials after 1893. This suggests that some inland bills in this period were drawn for short-term capital exports and were in the nature of finance bills. This would hardly be surprising, for if interest rates abroad were higher than in London English financiers could draw bills on some London banks in order to obtain funds to send abroad. Such bills would have been inland bills, but in fact they would have been the instruments for international short-term capital movements.

As is evident, these points have implications beyond the immediate subject of this research. They invite discussion in connection with such problems as the international movement of short-term capital before the First World War, the efficacy of Bank rate and the functioning of the international gold standard. Such discussion is not undertaken here, because another book would have to be written on the subject and the problem has already been tackled by many people, including Neisser, Morgenstern, Bloomfield, Beach and Ford. Here we should be content with the confirmation that the correlation of bills and interest rates displayed a radical change after the middle of the nineteenth century. This change suggests that, while commercial bills ('real bills', if we borrow the antiquated terminology of the Bullion Committee) predominated in the mid-nineteenth century, finance bills came into more prominence after the seventies, when telegraphs connected the money markets of the world.

2 CHANGES IN THE STRUCTURE OF SHORT-TERM INTEREST RATES

As has been shown in §1, in the mid-nineteenth century the amounts of bills drawn had a markedly positive correlation with interest rates. This probably shows that the drawers of bills largely disregarded the interest cost of bill finance, or that they were motivated by other considerations as well as by rates of discount. As has been suggested, most of the bills

Even in the depression it was more difficult to come to the decision to invest capital in Germany which was paying higher interest. Naturally, this withholding brought about a relative heightening of the sterling exchanges above the level of discount rate differentials.')
H. Neisser, 'Der internationale Geldmarkt vor und nach dem Kriege', *Weltwirtschaftliches Archiv*, XXIX$_2$, 1929, p. 222.

in this period were commercial bills, the drawings of which were principally influenced by the expectations of profits. As the movement of expected rates of profit is more volatile than that of interest rates, the former will normally exceed the latter in a boom, even if interest rates are at a high level. Conversely, in a depression, in spite of the lower level of interest rates, the expected profit rates will be at a still lower level. Thus, it seems natural for the amount of commercial bills to have a positive correlation with interest rates.

On the other hand, after the seventies bills tended to have less and less positive correlation with interest rates, suggesting that there came into being a large admixture of finance bills. As these bills are drawn for the purpose of international interest arbitrage, the prime concern of their drawers is the interest cost.

Now, such a difference in the character of both kinds of bills will be reflected in the different behaviour of the movements of interest rates as well as in the different structures of the short-term interest rates. Where commercial bills predominate discount rates are likely to experience violent fluctuations. In a boom, in spite of a rise in discount rates, there will be an increase in bill drawing which will push them up still further. In a depression the reverse will happen. On the other hand, where finance bills constitute the major part of the bills, the fluctuations of the discount rates would be confined within narrower limits. When the rates go up, the amount of bills would diminish, bringing them down again, and when the rates go down beyond a certain point, more bills would be drawn, which would push the rates up.

Moreover, after the seventies, when more and more nations adopted the gold standard and telegraphs connected the major money markets of the world, money would come in from other money markets when London rates went up. Although there was a broad parallelism in the movements of interest rates in the major countries of the world in pre-1914 years, inflows of foreign money in response to higher rates in London would have prevented an undue rise in money rates. Thus after 1866 the market rate of discount for three months' bank bills never reached 8·00 % in any month of the period up to the outbreak of the First World War. After 1873 the highest point it reached was 6·45 % in November 1907.

The relationship between the discount rate of shorter-term bills and that of longer-term bills, too, would be different. As drawers and discounters of finance bills are extremely sensitive to interest rates, they will switch freely between the shorter-term and longer-term markets, seeking the most advantageous terms. In such shifting between markets expectations about the future levels of discount rates play a decisive role. When higher rates are expected, borrowers hurry to draw long-term (say six months) paper and lenders prefer to discount short-term (say three months) paper. Thus, the discount rate for six months' bills tends to go up, while that for three months' bills tends to be depressed. When lower rates are expected in the future, the reverse will happen. As these expectations are influenced by the market's idea of the normal level of discount rates, it will usually happen that when the general level of short-term interest rates is low, the six months' rate is much higher than the three months' rate, and that when interest rates are higher than usual, the three months' rate is higher than the six months' rate.[1]

In the mid-nineteenth century, when commercial bills were dominant in the market, such a thing probably did not happen. As has been pointed out, drawers of commercial bills were not sensitive to changes (expected or real) in interest rates. Moreover, drawers of commercial bills could not freely move from one market to another. If they wanted to draw six months' bills, there had to be a good reason to do so, as, for example, that they exported their goods to distant places, such as India. Otherwise, six months' bills would have been regarded as accommodation paper. The relative amounts of exports to these distant markets might increase or decrease according to the circumstances of the times, but there is no theoretical ground to suppose that they would decrease in a boom, thus causing a diminution in the amount of six months' bills which would in turn depress the discount rate of these bills relative to that of three months' bills. (It is more likely that exports to distant markets would have increased in a boom, for the following reasons: the more distant the market, the longer it would take for reports of a glutted market to arrive: there may have been speculators who exported to such markets for the sole purpose of drawing six months' bills in order to continue their speculation with the money raised by discounting them.[2] Thus if we take exports to the three distant regions of Asia, Australia and Latin America, they amounted to £28·5 m. in 1855, or 30 % of the total exports of the U.K. in that year. They increased to £40·7 m. or 33 % of the total in 1857. If we compare 1860 with 1866, exports to the three distant markets increased from £48·3 m. to £66·6 m., while total exports increased from £135·9 m. to £188·9 m. Their proportion to total exports, therefore, showed almost no change, being 36 % in 1860 and 35 % in 1866.)[3]

We have, therefore, no reason to suppose that the relationship between the rate for three months' bills and that for six months' bills changed at the height of a boom, when their levels were higher than usual, from that which prevailed when their levels were lower. Un-

---

[1] The argument here is largely based upon F. W. Paish, *Long-Term and Short-Term Interest Rates in the United Kingdom*, Manchester, 1966.

[2] *The Economist*, of 9 November 1878, p. 1315, referred to the practice of exporting to distant markets for the purpose of raising money. (This passage is quoted on p. 38 above.)

[3] The figures of exports have been taken from B. R. Mitchell and P. Deane, *Abstract of British Historical Statistics*, Cambridge, 1962, Tables 3 and 12 in Chapter XI.

fortunately, we have at present not enough data to test this point, for *The Economist* began to publish the discount rate of six months' bills regularly only from November 1861. Thus we can observe the relationship between the two rates during the course of only one major cycle before 1870. From Table 30 it is seen that at the peaks of the rates the six months' bill rate is usually below the three months' rate, and the day-to-day money rate is always below both rates, save one exception, June 1867.

It must, however, be pointed out that by the sixties there was already a considerable amount of international short-term capital in Europe which flowed from one monetary centre to another, performing interest and exchange arbitrage, especially between London and Paris. For example, *The Economist* of 3 February 1866 reports that 'There is a very unusual amount of French money in London. This is now invested in short-dated bills becoming due, and renewed or not renewed according to the rate.'[1] Such Continental money competed for six months' bills after the panic of the year in early May. According to *The Economist* of 26 May 1866, 'Nevertheless, orders from abroad are still received for English paper of the best houses. As a very limited amount only, compared with the demand, moderate as it is for this class of bills, is to be had, the rate undergoes a proportionate reduction, and takers bid from $8\frac{1}{2}$ to 8 % for 6 months unexceptionable paper.'[2]

There is not any reference to foreign money taking bills up in *The Economist* of 1856–7. The period of high interest rates in 1864–6 was, therefore, not a typical boom period of the pre-seventies era, as far as the money market was concerned. In fact it already embodied a feature of the future international gold standard.[3] In spite of this, we must note that the inversion of the two discount rates (i.e. a situation in which the three months' bill rate is higher than six months' bill rate) occurred only at very high rates. It occurred at higher levels than 6·5 %, with one exception, September 1866.

After the seventies we see a very different picture. The difference can be summarized in the following three points:

(1) The extent of fluctuation in the rates is much narrower: the three

---

[1] *Ibid.*, p. 121.

[2] *The Economist*, p. 604. Similar references to foreign money taking bills up can be found in *The Economist* of 1864–6 at the following places: 17 September 1864, p. 1165; 24 September 1864, p. 1203; 31 October 1865, p. 1265; 19 May 1866, p. 593. Incidentally, such foreign money flowed out of Britain in a typically hot money fashion in May 1866 when Peel's Act was suspended, which foreigners are said to have confounded with the suspension of the gold standard. See 'A Practical View of the Act of 1844', *The Economist*, 29 December 1866. Bagehot, too, made a brief comment on this. See W. Bagehot, *Lombard Street*, London, 8th ed., 1882, p. 34.

[3] E. V. Morgan writes that high rates of interest attracted foreign short-term funds in the 1850s, but that such movements became an everyday occurrence only after the 1860s and 1870s. See Morgan, *Theory and Practice*, p. 189.

months' bill rate moved from 9·60 % (June 1866) to 1·31 % (October 1867) in the business cycle of the sixties, while at the peak and trough of the next cycle it went up to 7·31 % (November 1873) and down to 0·91 % (October 1876). In the eighties the peak was 5·13 % (February 1882) and the trough was 0·83 % (June 1885). In the nineties they were 5·69 % (November 1890) and 0·56 % (September and October 1894). At the turn of the century they were 6·13 % (December 1899) and 1·73 % (July 1905). In the boom and collapse of 1907–8 they were 6·45 % (November 1907) and 1·27 % (July 1908). (We cannot discern a clear peak and trough for the years immediately preceding 1914.)

(2) The inversion of the two kinds of discount rates began to appear at comparatively low levels of interest rates: in the seventies this occurred when the three months' bill rate was as low as 3·38 %, in March 1876. In the eighties this took place when it was only 2·45 %, in March 1887. In the nineties the lowest point at which this happened was 1·17 %, in March 1895 (this is the lowest record ever of such inversion).

(3) Not only the three months' bill rate, but also the rate of interest for day-to-day money began not infrequently to exceed the six months' bill rate.

All these new features combined to show that the movements and the interrelationship of rates came to be strongly influenced by the drawing of finance paper and the international movement of short-term capital. We must note moreover that, if finance bills came to predominate in the supply of bills, changes in the amount of bills would have ceased to be a determinant of discount rates; on the contrary, the drawing of bills would have become dependent upon changes in the latter. The levels of discount rates would have been determined by such factors as fluctuations in the amount of call or short notice money released by banks to the discount market (which again would have been determined by changes in the amounts of the banks' deposits and advances), demand for money from the Stock Exchange and the operations of the authorities. All these influences would have been reflected in the movements of the rates of interest of various kinds of short loan fund. Such was not the case before the seventies, when discount rates experienced violent fluctuations and when other short-term interest rates were mainly determined by the levels of discount rates. This can probably be proved by the fact that the day-to-day money rate virtually never exceeded discount rates in the sixties (there was one exception in June 1867, but this was probably accidental as it happened at low levels of discount rates, 2·28 % for three months' bills). On the other hand, after the seventies the day-to-day money rate very often was higher than discount rates by considerable margins. Of course expectations about the future course of interest rates played a part in this. But was this not due also to the fact that they were influenced by such independent variables as enumerated above, and does this not show that the day-to-day rate was influencing discount rates rather than *vice versa*? This point, however, will not be examined in more detail. In order to prove it, it would be necessary to explore matters other than those encompassed by this study, such as the behaviour of the capital market, of the banks and of the authorities in this period.

CONCLUSIONS

If 'conclusion' be a recapitulation of that which has been stated in the foregoing pages, it could well be omitted. Instead, I am tempted to expatiate on what I have had in mind but have not been able to put in the preceding chapters because of the difficulty of proof.

An eternal trap for historians is the temptation to project the present into the past. That the commercial world of the first two-thirds of the nineteenth century was totally different from that of the present day is well known. What such differences mean in terms of money and banking, however, seems not to have been studied very closely. As far as merchanting is concerned, the biggest differences between the present and past probably lies in the field of communication and transportation. Lack of telegraphs in earlier years meant that nobody was sure where supply could be found and where demand was. In such a world merchants played a much more important role than in the present and concentrated both demand and supply in their hands. Either they accumulated a large stockpile of goods and waited for the orders to come or they sent the goods to some prospective markets without knowing precisely the state of the demand there for the goods. *The Statist* of 8 August 1903 explained the circumstance thus,

One of the consequences of the beneficent invention [telegraph]..., is that the great merchant of former times has become unnecessary, and therefore is rapidly ceasing to exist. In the old times it was so uncertain when goods would be received that it was absolutely essential to keep large stocks always on hand; therefore great merchants with very immense capitals grew up, owning vast warehouses in which valuables of all kinds were stored for gradual use.[1]

Not only was the supply of goods unstable, but the receipt of cash in payment was often very unreliable. A Birmingham merchant, A. W. Keep, described the conditions of trade with Australia towards the end of the seventies as follows,

Mail day then was once a month. Every fourth week we got—or were supposed to get—a mail in from Australia and New Zealand, which occasionally arrived to time, but which more often didn't. When it came it sometimes brought a good deal of money which had been anxiously awaited. Very often, however, the mail was a disappointing one. Plenty of orders, but very little cash, and then many anxious hours were spent in deciding whether So-and-so's orders should be put in hand or held over until his promised remittances arrived.[2]

A merchant firm relying on mails once every four weeks would be inconceivable today, and from this we can get an idea of how different commercial activities were in the middle years of the nineteenth

[1] 'Preferential Treatment of the Colonies', *The Statist*, 8 August 1903, p. 268.
[2] A. W. Keep, 'Sixty Years in Business: A Birmingham Merchant's Recollections of Old Time Methods' (a reprint from *Birmingham Mail* of 1936, in Birmingham Public Library).

century. To this lack of telegraph was added the slowness and uncertainty of transport by sailing vessels. Thus it was necessary for several
merchant firms to intervene between the producer and the final
consumer, providing a cushion, so to speak, when the supply failed. Not
only merchants, but also manufacturers, were probably forced to
maintain a large inventory of raw materials if they wanted to ensure the
smooth working of their factories, because of the uncertainty of the
supply.

Thus inventory investment appears to have played a much more
important part than in the present day and the financing of these goods
in store must have been a great burden on the money market. On the
other hand, the banking habit was not developed among the general
public and much money must have been circulating outside the banking
system. It is no wonder then that the demand for money was so strong
compared with the supply of it that the discounts plus advances/deposits
ratios of banks in industrial districts were normally far in excess of
100 %. This, of course, forced banks to accommodate their customers
mainly by discounting of bills.

Such a state of affairs gradually came to an end after the seventies.
Telegraphs and steamers did away with both the enormous amount of
inventory of goods and the middlemen merchants. Branch banking
absorbed money into the banking system. Thus, the demand for money
for inventory financing dwindled and the supply of money increased,
enabling banks to lend in the form of overdrafts, which in turn caused
bills to decline.

George Lord, a Manchester merchant, gave the following evidence
before the Royal Commission on Depression of Trade and Industry,
1886:

I think that at the present time there is some prospect of revival. We find, for instance, that
in the large Indian markets the stocks are very light; my table L gives plain cottons 1,970,000
pieces as against 3,254,000 at the end of the preceding year. Not only are they light at the ports
of India, but the intermediate supplies between the ports and consuming districts are light,
and owing to the extension of railways and the telegraph, now the dealers hold very light
supplies compared with what they did in former days, and many of the merchants keep
entirely free from stocks. They work largely now on account of the native dealers, and only
ship exactly what is ordered, that, to a large extent, is one of the causes, as I take it, of the
depression being felt, because the dispensing with those stocks and intermediate supplies
whilst the telegraph and the steamer have been doing their work since; in fact, the opening
of the Suez Canal, has been equivalent for the time being whilst the process has been going
on, to an increase of production, having the intermediate supplies thrown on to the customers.
I should say that process has gone nearly as far as it can go, and from that circumstance I hope
for some future improvement.[1]

[1] Royal Commission on Depression of Trade and Industry, 1886, Minutes of Evidence,
Q. 5278, BPP 1886, Vol. 21.
    Incidentally, the railways earlier exerted the same influences on the level of inventory
goods held by domestic traders in the forties. George Carr Glyn gave the following evidence

This seems logical enough, but it would be very difficult to prove that it was true. Lord's table L means nothing in this respect: it only records the change over one year of the amount of stocks of cotton piece goods, whereas the tendency for the levels of inventory goods to decrease is a secular one. Moreover, as prices were tumbling in the eighties, everybody would have avoided an unnecessary accumulation of stocks of goods. Thus secular change would have been inseparably intertwined with cyclical change. Even so, there cannot be any doubt that telegraphs, steamers and the Suez Canal brought about a revolutionary change in the general level of inventories.

Thus, the decline in the use of inland commercial bills was a reflection of the reduction in the general level of inventories of goods, which was caused by the revolution in communication and transport after the seventies of the nineteenth century. After inland commercial bills declined, the bill market was dominated by foreign finance bills drawn for the international movement of short-term capital, which was again made possible by telegraphs.

before the Select Committee on Commercial Distress, 1848: '1649...I am certain that as every Ten or Twenty Miles of Railway were opened a very large quantity of fixed Capital was released, by enabling the Shopkeepers in all the Towns to hold comparatively short Stocks of Goods...' '1651. They carry on Business more from Hand to Mouth?—Yes, they do.' '1652. Can you form any thing like an Estimate of the Amount to which Capital has been so released?—I have tried to do so, but it is almost impossible to arrive at a Calculation. My Knowledge of the Fact is derived from Questions that I have put to some large Dealers in some of the principal Towns, and they all concurred in this Result.' (Select Committee on Commercial Distress, 1848, *Minutes of Evidence*, Session 1, Vol. 2.)

Table 1. Numbers of bank offices in England and Wales, 1855–1913

Years	Joint-stock banks			Country private banks			London private banks			Total banks		
	No. of banks (a)	No. of offices (b)	(b)/(a) (c)	No. of banks (a)	No. of offices (b)	(b)/(a) (c)	No. of banks (a)	No. of offices (b)	(b)/(a) (c)	No. of banks (a)	No. of offices (b)	(b)/(a) (c)
1855	100	631	6·3	252	492	2·0	57	62	1·1	409	1,185	2·9
1856	98	639	6·5	250	489	2·0	57	64	1·1	405	1,192	2·9
1857	98	659	6·7	237	490	2·1	56	62	1·1	391	1,211	3·1
1858	97	651	6·7	246	493	2·0	56	62	1·1	399	1,206	3·0
1859	97	658	6·8	247	497	2·0	54	60	1·1	398	1,215	3·1
1860	97	670	6·9	246	493	2·0	54	60	1·1	397	1,223	3·1
1861	98	681	6·9	240	487	2·0	51	57	1·1	389	1,225	3·1
1862	107	724	6·8	239	500	2·1	51	57	1·1	397	1,281	3·2
1863	114	827	7·3	239	508	2·1	51	56	1·1	404	1,391	3·4
1864	117	948	8·1	232	521	2·2	46	51	1·1	395	1,520	3·8
1865	118	1,018	8·6	219	514	2·3	45	50	1·1	382	1,582	4·1
1866	116	1,013	8·7	212	520	2·5	43	48	1·1	371	1,581	4·3
1867	117	1,031	8·8	214	523	2·4	42	47	1·1	373	1,601	4·3
1868	120	1,058	8·8	209	524	2·5	41	46	1·1	370	1,628	4·4
1869	118	1,056	8·9	207	524	2·5	41	46	1·1	366	1,626	4·4
1870	117	1,063	9·1	206	518	2·5	42	47	1·1	365	1,628	4·5
1871	117	1,077	9·2	204	523	2·6	42	47	1·1	363	1,647	4·5
1872	122	1,128	9·2	203	528	2·6	43	48	1·1	368	1,704	4·6
1873	124	1,201	9·7	198	524	2·6	44	48	1·1	366	1,773	4·8
1874	122	1,277	10·5	197	529	2·7	44	48	1·1	363	1,854	5·1
1875	127	1,376	10·8	190	539	2·8	43	47	1·1	360	1,962	5·5
1876	125	1,447	11·6	188	550	2·9	43	47	1·1	356	2,044	5·7
1877	124	1,504	12·1	185	553	3·0	43	47	1·1	352	2,104	6·0
1878	124	1,540	12·4	179	556	3·1	42	46	1·1	345	2,142	6·2
1879	125	1,552	12·4	175	566	3·2	42	46	1·1	342	2,164	6·3
1880	128	1,600	12·5	170	555	3·3	43	47	1·1	341	2,202	6·3
1881	127	1,642	12·9	168	564	3·4	43	50	1·2	338	2,256	6·5
1882	127	1,685	13·3	168	573	3·4	43	52	1·2	338	2,310	6·7
1883	123	1,724	14·0	163	584	3·6	43	52	1·2	329	2,360	7·2
1884	119	1,754	14·7	160	596	3·7	40	49	1·2	319	2,399	7·5

Table 1 (continued)

Years	Joint-stock banks			Country private banks			London private banks			Total banks		
	No. of banks (a)	No. of offices (b)	(b)/(a) (c)	No. of banks (a)	No. of offices (b)	(b)/(a) (c)	No. of banks (a)	No. of offices (b)	(b)/(a) (c)	No. of banks (a)	No. of offices (b)	(b)/(a) (c)
1885	120	1,814	15·1	160	598	3·7	39	48	1·2	319	2,460	7·7
1886	121	1,863	15·4	159	602	3·8	39	48	1·2	319	2,513	7·9
1887	118	1,930	16·4	157	606	3·9	39	48	1·2	314	2,584	8·2
1888	119	1,997	16·8	147	606	4·1	38	49	1·3	304	2,652	8·7
1889	117	2,205	18·8	140	600	4·3	40	51	1·3	297	2,856	9·6
1890	113	2,385	21·1	129	586	4·5	39	50	1·2	281	3,021	10·8
1891	113	2,605	23·1	115	567	4·9	33	41	1·3	261	3,213	12·3
1892	109	2,741	25·1	109	567	5·2	29	37	1·3	247	3,345	13·5
1893	108	2,863	26·5	104	553	5·3	28	37	1·3	240	3,453	14·4
1894	102	2,978	29·2	97	554	5·7	26	42	1·6	225	3,574	15·9
1895	102	3,660	30·0	94	558	5·9	26	43	1·7	222	3,661	16·5
1896	99	3,381	34·2	76	387	5·1	25	33	1·3	200	3,801	19·0
1897	95	3,592	37·8	71	336	4·7	25	33	1·3	191	3,961	20·7
1898	89	3,825	43·0	68	345	5·1	24	32	1·3	181	4,202	23·2
1899	86	4,038	47·0	67	356	5·3	24	32	1·3	177	4,426	25·0
1900	83	4,212	50·7	59	329	5·6	22	29	1·3	164	4,570	27·9
1901	78	4,387	56·2	55	310	5·6	21	29	1·4	154	4,726	30·7
1902	72	4,579	63·6	42	284	6·8	20	28	1·4	134	4,891	36·5
1903	66	4,741	71·8	37	234	6·3	20	28	1·4	123	5,003	40·7
1904	63	4,830	76·7	34	222	6·5	18	26	1·4	115	5,078	44·2
1905	61	4,995	81·9	30	216	7·2	18	26	1·4	109	5,237	48·0
1906	57	5,118	89·8	28	195	7·0	18	25	1·4	103	5,338	51·8
1907	55	5,263	95·7	26	190	7·3	17	24	1·4	98	5,477	55·8
1908	54	5,520	102·2	23	159	6·9	17	25	1·5	94	5,704	60·7
1909	52	5,583	107·4	21	153	7·3	15	23	1·5	88	5,759	65·4
1910	50	5,760	115·2	20	150	7·5	14	20	1·4	84	5,930	70·6
1911	47	5,962	126·9	19	150	7·9	13	15	1·2	79	6,127	77·6
1912	43	6,140	142·8	18	144	8·0	12	14	1·2	73	6,298	86·3
1913	41	6,426	156·7	17	133	7·8	12	14	1·2	70	6,573	93·9

Note: Number of offices includes head offices, branches, sub-branches, agencies and sub-agencies, but not London agencies of country banks.
Source: *Banking Almanac.*

Appendix to Table 1

Sykes, *Amalgamation Movement*, p. 113, states that the number of bank branches in England and Wales was as follows:

Years	Number of branches	Years	Number of branches
1851	96 (H. T. Easton)	1896	3,959
1858	1,195 (R. H. I. Palgrave)	1901	4,762
1872	1,779	1906	5,433
1881	2,413	1911	6,267
1886	2,716	1913	6,839
1891	3,383	—	—

Sykes says that these figures are quoted from *Banking Almanac*. In the 'Introductory Remarks to Banking Directory' in each issue of *Banking Almanac* statistics of the number of bank offices are given. Sykes probably used the figures shown there. These are as follows:

Years (31 Oct.)	Number of offices	Years	Number of offices
1872	1,779	1901	4,872
1881	2,302	1906	5,528
1886	2,936	1911	6,255
1891	3,628	1913	6,844
1896	3,941		

Sykes gives for 1872 the same number of bank offices, not branches, as *Banking Almanac*. It is not clear how he reached the figure of 2,413 for the year 1881. *Banking Almanac* of this year does not give the number of offices, but the Almanac of 1904 gave the figure retrospectively as 2,302. The figure given by him for 1886 is equally mysterious. The figure for 1891 seems to have been obtained by adding 15 (the number of offices in the Isle of Man) to 3,628 and then subtracting the number of head offices of banks in that year (which is 261 according to my counting). Sykes' figure of 3,383 is, therefore, the number of bank branches in England and Wales and the Isle of Man. His figure for 1896, then, was apparently obtained by adding 18 (the number of offices in the Isle of Man) to 3,941 given by the Almanac for England and Wales. His figure of 3,959 is, therefore, the number of bank offices (not branches) in England and Wales and the Isle of Man. His other figures defy understanding, too.

The number of bank offices given by *Banking Almanac* is not an adequate basis for such enumeration. As has been pointed out in Chapter 1, it does not discriminate between genuine banks and other financial institutions in London, so that the number of bank offices given by the *Almanac* is inflated by their inclusion. If Sykes calculated the number of bank branches by subtracting from it the number of head offices of joint-stock banks and private banks, the result obtained is indeed imperfect.

Table 2. Banks with more than 100 offices, 1874–1913

Years	London & County Banking Co.	National Provincial Bank of England	Capital & Counties Bank	London & Provincial Bank	Lloyds Bank	Midland Bank	Metropolitan Bank	London & South-Western Bank	Barclays Bank	Wilts & Dorset Banking Co.	Parr's Bank	York City & County Bank
1874	149	138										
1875	150	137										
1876	152	143										
1877	156	145										
1878	156	145										
1879	156	148										
1880	158	150										
1881	158	152										
1882	162	153										
1883	162	152										
1884	162	152										
1885	162	155										
1886	162	156										
1887	165	156	101									
1888	170	156	104									
1889	171	165	116	105								
1890	174	168	133	115	130							
1891	174	168	162	119	145							
1892	176	212	170	128	175							
1893	175	215	171	126	185		115					
1894	176	216	179	140	191	105	120	101				
1895	177	218	186	144	199	110	121	101				
1896	177	219	213	150	205	146	122	109	201			
1897	182	230	226	148	249	162	129	113	226	124		
1898	184	233	256	172	256	202	131	124	229	124	108	103
1899	186	241	270	190	279	249	134	128	242	128	118	112
1900	191	250	290	197	309	284	133	134	266	131	130	145
1901	198	261	319	203	319	317	135	140	272	136	139	161
1902	219	266	326	217	344	357	138	147	317	145	156	164
1903	229	283	354	229	408	430	137	148	319	148	160	165
1904	239	295	376	232	418	440	137	152	348	150	163	168
1905	246	299	389	237	450	447	137	158	401	152	167	177
1906	255	304	400	239	517	485	138	160	429	157	168	180
1907	264	308	415	248	527	495	140	166	453	160	170	186
1908	268	316	428	255	560	618	140	171	464	166	175	
1909		326	433	272	581	649	149	178	481	167	189	
1910		339	439	292	595	680	158	179	490	171	264	
1911		356	459	300	621	704	161	184	547	177	267	
1912		390	470	320	639	725	161	191	564	182	273	
1913		419	481	344	673	846	166	195	599	182	277	

Table 2 (continued)

Years	Union Bank of London	Lancashire & Yorkshire Bank	Manchester & Liverpool District Banking Co.	North & South Wales Bank	United Counties Bank	Bank of Liverpool (Martins Bank)	Williams Deacon's Bank	Manchester & County Bank	London Joint Stock Bank	London & Westminster Bank	North-Eastern Banking Co.	Union Bank of Manchester
1874												
1875												
1876												
1877												
1878												
1879												
1880												
1881												
1882												
1883												
1884												
1885												
1886												
1887												
1888												
1889												
1890												
1891												
1892												
1893												
1894												
1895												
1896												
1897												
1898												
1899												
1900												
1901												
1902												
1903	145											
1904	150	117	101	100								
1905	152	118	108	102	148	126						
1906	163	121	111	103	156	128						
1907	175	121	118	105	185	127	100	100				
1908	179	122	184	110	189	129	102	102				
1909	185	126	194		197	130	104	103	233	305		
1910	194	128	197		200	139	106	105	247	316	100	
1911	200	129	201		203	139	110	107	273	337	99	
1912	208	131	204		207	140	110	110	285	345	99	
1913	215	131	209		207	139	115	115	302	358	100	101

NOTE: National Provincial Bank had had more than 100 offices since 1856. London & County Banking Co. had had more than 100 offices since 1859.
SOURCE: Banking Almanac.

Table 3. Scale of stamp duties on bills of exchange and
promissory notes*

†Inland bills drawn in Great Britain, 1815–42, in the U.K., 1842–54			†Inland bills drawn in Ireland, 1815–42	
Amount of bills	Short date (Less than 2 months)	Long date (More than 2 months)	Amount of bills	Amount of duty
£2 and not exceeding £5. 5s.	1s. 0d.	1s. 6d.	Not exceeding £10	0s. 6d.
£5. 5s. to £20	1s. 6d.	2s. 0d.	£10 to £30	1s. 6d.
£20 to £30	2s. 0d.	2s. 6d.	£30 to £50	2s. 0d.
£30 to £50	2s. 6d.	3s. 6d.	£50 to £100	3s. 0d.
£50 to £100	3s. 6d.	4s. 6d.	£100 to £200	4s. 0d.
£100 to £200	4s. 6d.	5s. 0d.	£200 to £500	5s. 0d.
£200 to £300	5s. 0d.	6s. 0d.	£500 to £1,000	8s. 0d.
£300 to £500	6s. 0d.	8s. 6d.	£1,000 to £3,000	15s. 0d.
£500 to £1,000	8s. 6d.	12s. 6d.	Above £3,000	25s. 0d.
£1,000 to £2,000	12s. 6d.	15s. 0d.		
£2,000 to £3,000	15s. 0d.	25s. 0d.		
Above £3,000	25s. 0d.	30s. 0d.		

* Promissory notes payable on demand under £100 are regarded as bank notes.
† Bills drawn in foreign countries on the U.K. were not assessed to stamp duty. But bills drawn in the U.K. on foreign were assessed to the duty and when they were drawn in a set of three or more a special rate of duty (at about one-third of the ordinary rate) was applied, which is not reproduced here.
SOURCE: Commissioners of Inland Revenue, 1856–69, *Report*, BPP 1870, Vol. 20, pp. 501–2.

Table 4. Amounts of bills drawn estimated by W. Leatham
(inland bills only)

Calendar years	(figures in £ thousands) Bills drawn in Great Britain	Bills drawn in Ireland	Bills drawn in the U.K.
1815	477,493		
1824	232,430		
1825	260,379		
July 1826 to June 1827	207,347		
1832			356,153
1833			383,660
1834			379,155
1835	294,775	51,109	345,884
1836	355,289	59,155	414,444
1837	333,269	54,179	387,448
1838	341,947	54,359	396,306
1839	394,203	55,616	449,819

SOURCE: For 1815, 1824, 1825 and July 1826 to June 1827, Leatham, (*First Series*) *Letters*, pp. 67–8; for 1832–4, Leatham, (*Second Series*) *Letters*, p. 34; for 1835–9, Leatham, (*First Series*) *Letters*, pp. 67–8.

Table 5. Summary result of questionnaires sent to five banking houses by W. Newmarch in 1849

Class of stamps	Number of bills	Average usance of bills (months)	Total amount of bills ($£$)	Average amount of bills ($£$)
1s.	—	—	—	—
1s. 6d.	138	2	2,095	15·2
2s.	323	2·9	6,215	19·2
2s. 6d.	464	3·1	13,438	28·9
(I)	925	2·7	21,748	21·1
3s. 6d.	570	3·3	26,292	46·1
4s. 6d.	630	3·7	47,096	74·7
5s.	366	3·6	57,472	157·0
6s.	298	3·8	84,645	284·0
(II)	1,864	3·6	215,505	140·4
8s. 6d.	358	3·9	153,429	428·5
12s. 6d.	227	4·0	181,715	800·5
15s.	100	4·1	149,727	1,497·2
25s.	27	4·1	70,127	2,597·3
30s.	32	4·0	144,189	4,505·8
(III)	744	3·8	699,187	1,965·8
(I) + (II) + (III)	3,533	3·4	936,440	265·0
Foreign bills	834	3·2	280,444	336·2
Total	4,367	3·4	1,216,884	278·6

SOURCE: Newmarch, 'An Attempt...', p. 150.

Table 6. Amounts of inland bills drawn in Great Britain (estimated by Newmarch)

	(figures in $£$ millions)		
Calendar years	Amounts of bills	Calendar years	Amounts of bills
1828	286	1838	345
1829	278	1839	399
1830	261	1840	411
1831	288	1841	381
1832	255	1842	327
1833	284	1843	309
1834	277	1844	321
1835	296	1845	374
1836	373	1846	397
1837	335	1847	399

Figures are calculated from Newmarch's table in 'An Attempt...', p. 175, on the assumption that the average usance of bills was 3·4 months.

Table 7. *The rate of stamp duty on bills of exchange and promissory notes, 10 October 1854–31 December 1870*

Inland bills*		Foreign bills†	
Face value of bills	Amount of duty	Face value of bills	Amount of duty
Not exceeding £5	0s. 1d.	Not exceeding £25	0s. 1d.
£5 to £10	0s. 2d.	£25 to £50	0s. 2d.
£10 to £25	0s. 3d.	£50 to £75	0s. 3d.
£25 to £50	0s. 6d.	£75 to £100	0s. 4d.
£50 to £75	0s. 9d.	£100 to £200	0s. 8d.
£75 to £100	1s. 0d.	£200 to £300	1s. 0d.
£100 to £200	2s. 0d.	£300 to £400	1s. 4d.
£200 to £300	3s. 0d.	£400 to £500	1s. 8d.
£300 to £400	4s. 0d.	£500 to £750	2s. 6d.
£400 to £500	5s. 0d.	£750 to £1,000	3s. 4d.
£500 to £750	7s. 6d.	£1,000 to £1,500	5s. 0d.
£750 to £1,000	10s. 0d.	£1,500 to £2,000	6s. 8d.
£1,000 to £1,500	15s. 0d.	£2,000 to £3,000	10s. 0d.
£1,500 to £2,000	20s. 0d.	£3,000 to £4,000	13s. 4d.
£2,000 to £3,000	30s. 0d.	Exceeding £4,000‡	15s. 0d.
£3,000 to £4,000	40s. 0d.		
Exceeding £4,000‡	45s. 0d.		

* Rates for inland bills are also applied to foreign bills drawn out of but payable in the U.K.

† These rates are applied to bills drawn in but payable out of the U.K., when they are drawn in sets of three or more. Each bill (whether original or duplicate) in a set is to carry a stamp at these rates.

‡ After 1861 beyond £4,000, for every £1,000 or fraction of £1,000: inland bills, 10s.; foreign bills, 3s. 4d.

SOURCE: Commissioners of Inland Revenue, 1856–69, *Report*, BPP 1870, Vol. 20, p. 124.

Table 8. Summary result of analysis of 1,400 inland bills collected by Palgrave

Class of stamp	Number of bills	Average usance of bills (months)	Total amount of bills (£)	Average amount of bills (£)
1d.	—	—	—	—
2d.	39	2·8	342	8·7
3d.	315	3·2	5,343	16·7
6d.	241	3·2	8,453	35·0
(I)	595	2·8	14,138	23·8
9d.	87	3·4	5,236	60·2
1s.	67	3·5	5,850	87·3
2s.	92	3·5	13,457	146·2
3s.	71	3·5	20,698	291·5
(II)	317	3·5	45,241	142·7
4s.	63	3·1	22,295	353·9
5s.	59	3·3	28,234	478·5
7s. 6d.	15	3·5	8,496	566·4
10s.	11	4·0	7,150	650·0
15s.	153	4·3	140,446	918·0
20s.	134	4·1	200,749	1,498·1
30s.	29	4·1	76,038	2,622·0
40s.	8	5·6	29,386	3,673·2
Upwards of 40s.	16	4·1	75,863	4,741·4
(III)	488	4·0	588,657	1,206·3
Total (I) + (II) + (III)	1,400	4·1	648,036	462·9

SOURCE: Palgrave, *Notes on Banking*, p. 31.

Table 9. Estimated amounts of bills drawn, 1856–70 (by Palgrave)

		Foreign bills (figures in £ thousands)					
		England on Foreign		Foreign on Foreign	Foreign on England	Total foreign bills	Total inland and foreign bills
Years	Inland bills	on inland stamps	on foreign stamps				
1856	498,520						
1857	507,360						
1858	445,760						
1859	487,340	14,500	29,100	18,300	301,900	363,800	851,140
1860	537,200	17,100	34,200	21,500	355,900	428,700	965,900
1861	533,900	15,500	31,100	19,600	323,200	389,400	923,300
1862	538,440	16,700	33,500	21,000	347,300	418,500	956,940
1863	598,080	20,200	40,500	25,400	419,500	505,600	1,103,680
1864	676,474	24,000	48,100	30,200	498,900	601,200	1,277,674
1865	675,277	24,000	48,100	30,300	499,700	602,100	1,277,377
1866	670,421	22,000	44,100	27,700	457,900	551,700	1,222,121
1867	612,861	22,100*	42,200	27,700	445,000	537,000	1,149,861
1868	602,288	22,100	44,200	27,800	459,300	553,400	1,155,688
1869	604,415	23,600	47,200	29,800	490,400	591,000	1,195,415
1870	677,776	24,500	49,000	30,700	507,400	611,600	1,289,376

* Mistake of calculations.
Source: Palgrave, *Notes on Banking*, pp. 34, 39 and 42.

Table 10. Estimated amounts of bills* drawn, 1858–77 (by Barnett)

	(figures in £ thousands)		
Years	Amount of bills	Years	Amount of bills
1858	807,814	1868	1,199,659
1859	886,259	1869	1,242,717
1860	1,003,039	1870	1,365,566
1861	959,640	1871	1,512,458
1862	992,135	1872	1,711,188
1863	1,145,504	1873	1,759,303
1864	1,324,868	1874	1,617,984
1865	1,329,954	1875	1,529,671
1866	1,267,025	1876	1,373,564
1867	1,196,902	1877	1,372,981

* The breakdown between inland and foreign bills is not given.
Source: C. Barnett, *Effect of the Development of Banking Facilities*, p. 89.

Table 11. Estimated amounts of bills, 1855–70

(figures in £ millions)

Years	Inland bills					Foreign bills					Total of inland and foreign bills
	£0–75	£75–400	£400–3,000	Over £3,000	Total	£0–75	£75–400	£400–3,000	Over £3,000	Total	
1855	72	145	225	59	502	11	80	173	37	301	803
1856	80	165	254	66	564	13	92	223	54	380	944
1857	85	165	251	72	574	12	87	230	56	385	959
1858	86	150	206	55	496	12	86	205	47	350	846
1859	87	161	231	62	541	12	93	234	54	393	934
1860	96	170	250	65	581	17	106	275	57	454	1,035
1861	96	168	248	62	574	15	118	229	45	407	981
1862	98	170	249	61	578	16	140	229	49	434	1,012
1863	97	183	293	75	647	17	155	285	72	530	1,177
1864	100	195	342	104	742	19	172	339	107	636	1,378
1865	102	199	337	105	742	20	170	336	110	636	1,378
1866	104	203	337	85	729	21	171	297	90	578	1,306
1867	106	196	298	64	665	23	176	288	72	559	1,224
1868	105	197	295	55	652	23	181	295	76	576	1,228
1869	108	203	292	53	656	25	194	318	78	616	1,272
1870	108	204	352	57	721	23	199	344	81	647	1,368

NOTE: Because of rounding, totals do not necessarily agree with the sums of individual items.

Table 12. *The rate of stamp duty on bills of exchange and promissory notes, 1 January 1871–1914*

Face value of bills	Amount of duty	Face value of bills	Amount of duty
Not exceeding £5	0s. 1d.	£300 to £400	4s. 0d.
£5 to £10	0s. 2d.	£400 to £500	5s. 0d.
£10 to £25	0s. 3d.	£500 to £600	6s. 0d.
£25 to £50	0s. 6d.	£600 to £700	7s. 0d.
£50 to £75	0s. 9d.	£700 to £800	8s. 0d.
£75 to £100	1s. 0d.	£800 to £900	9s. 0d.
£100 to £200	2s. 0d.	£900 to £1,000	10s. 0d.
£200 to £300	3s. 0d.		

NOTE: Beyond £1,000, too, the rate is uniformly 1s. in £100.
SOURCE: BPP 1905, Vol. 24, p. 130.

Table 13. *Estimated amounts of bills, 1871–82*

	(figures in £ millions) Face values of bills				
Years	£0–75	£75–400	£400–3,000	Over £3,000	Total*
1871	131	441	771	178	1,521
1872	133	473	905	221	1,732
1873	136	483	944	217	1,781
1874	137	463	848	183	1,631
1875	141	452	777	164	1,533
1876	140	416	671	142	1,370
1877	145	413	664	145	1,367
1878	144	395	602	136	1,277
1879	134	380	598	149	1,261
1880	131	393	638	149	1,310
1881	128	403	656	159	1,345
1882	123	397	662	168	1,350

* Because of rounding, totals do not necessarily agree with the sums of individual items.

Table 14. *Estimated amounts of bills and revenue from stamps on bills, 1871–82*

Years	(figures in £ thousands) Estimated amounts of bills (a)	Revenue from stamps (b)	(a)/(b) (c)
1871	1,520,719	846	1,798
1872	1,732,042	959	1,806
1873	1,780,891	985	1,808
1874	1,631,060	903	1,806
1875	1,533,148	852	1,799
1876	1,369,910	769	1,781
1877	1,367,493	770	1,776
1878	1,277,373	723	1,767
1879	1,261,102	711	1,774
1880	1,310,478	740	1,771
1881	1,344,957	756	1,779
1882	1,350,175	758	1,781
Average	—	—	1,787

Table 15. *Estimated amounts of bills, 1855–1913*

(figures in £ millions)

Years	Inland bills	Foreign bills	Total*	Years	Inland bills	Foreign bills	Total*
1855	502	301	803	1885			1,170
1856	564	380	944	1886			1,148
1857	574	385	959	1887			1,184
1858	496	350	846	1888			1,255
1859	541	393	934	1889			1,330
1860	581	454	1,035	1890			1,351
1861	574	407	981	1891			1,276
1862	578	434	1,012	1892			1,190
1863	647	530	1,177	1893	516	642	1,158
1864	742	636	1,378	1894	490	630	1,121
1865	742	636	1,378	1895	505	699	1,204
1866	729	578	1,306	1896	510	686	1,197
1867	665	559	1,224	1897	517	666	1,183
1868	652	576	1,228	1898	505	690	1,194
1869	656	616	1,272	1899	516	744	1,260
1870	721	647	1,368	1900	507	733	1,240
1871			1,521	1901	499	756	1,255
1872			1,732	1902	512	741	1,252
1873			1,781	1903	501	734	1,235
1874			1,631	1904	510	744	1,254
1875			1,533	1905	538	846	1,384
1876			1,370	1906	562	918	1,480
1877			1,367	1907	586	965	1,551
1878			1,277	1908	529	883	1,412
1879			1,261	1909	543	926	1,469
1880			1,310	1910	571	977	1,548
1881			1,345	1911	585	1,020	1,605
1882			1,350	1912	609	1,124	1,732
1883			1,334	1913	651	1,203	1,854
1884			1,251				

* Because of rounding, totals do not necessarily agree with the sums of individual items.

Table 16. *Estimated proportions of foreign bills, 1871–82*

(% figures)

	Actual proportions of foreign bills				Trend values of proportions of foreign bills			
Years	in bills of £0–75	of £75–400	of £400–3,000	of £3,000 to ∞	of £0–75	of £75–400	of £400–3,000	of £3,000 to ∞
1855	13·5	35·6	43·4	38·9				
1856	13·5	35·7	46·8	44·8				
1857	12·3	34·4	47·8	43·6				
1858	12·7	36·4	49·9	46·2				
1859	12·2	36·6	50·4	46·6				
1860	14·8	38·0	52·3	46·8				
1861	13·5	41·3	48·0	42·2				
1862	14·1	45·2	47·9	44·5				
1863	15·2	45·9	49·3	49·3				
1864	16·0	46·8	49·7	50·6				
1865	16·8	46·1	49·9	51·1				
1866	16·6	45·7	46·8	51·4				
1867	17·5	47·3	49·1	52·8				
1868	18·2	47·9	50·0	58·1				
1869	19·0	48·9	52·1	59·4				
1870	17·5	49·5	49·4	58·4	18·35	50·85	50·55	57·80
1871					18·77	51·95	50·77	58·96
1872					19·19	53·05	50·99	60·12
1873					19·61	54·15	51·21	61·28
1874					20·03	55·25	51·43	62·44
1875					20·45	56·35	51·65	63·60
1876					20·87	57·45	51·87	64·76
1877					21·29	58·55	52·09	65·92
1878					21·71	59·65	52·31	67·08
1879					22·13	60·75	52·53	68·24
1880					22·55	61·85	52·75	69·40
1881					22·97	62·95	52·97	70·56
1882					23·39	64·05	53·19	71·72

Table 17. *Estimated amounts of foreign bills drawn, 1871–82*

(figures are in £ millions)

Years	£0–75	£75–400	£400–3,000	Over £3,000	Total* foreign bills	Inland bills	Total bills
1871	25	229	391	105	750	771	1,521
1872	26	251	462	133	871	861	1,732
1873	27	262	483	133	905	876	1,781
1874	28	256	436	115	834	797	1,631
1875	29	255	401	104	789	744	1,533
1876	29	239	348	92	709	661	1,370
1877	31	242	346	96	714	653	1,367
1878	31	236	315	92	673	604	1,277
1879	30	231	314	101	676	585	1,261
1880	30	243	337	103	712	598	1,310
1881	29	254	347	112	742	603	1,345
1882	29	254	352	121	756	594	1,350

* Because of rounding, totals do not necessarily agree with the sums of individual items.
Figures are estimated by extrapolation of linear trend values of ratios of foreign bills in each group of bills for 1855–70.

Table 18. *Net national income and amounts of bills, 1855–1913*

Years*	Net national income (a) (current prices)	Total bills drawn (b)	(b)/(a) × 100 (c)	Inland bills drawn (d)	(d)/(a) × 100 (e)
		(figures are in £ millions)			
1855	636	803	126	502	79
1856	665	944	142	564	85
1857	645	959	149	574	89
1858	635	846	133	496	78
1859	656	934	142	540	82
1860	694	1,035	149	581	84
1861	727	981	135	574	79
1862	741	1,012	137	578	78
1863	759	1,177	155	647	85
1864	795	1,378	173	742	93
1865	822	1,378	168	742	90
1866	846	1,306	154	729	86
1867	840	1,224	146	665	79
1868	836	1,228	147	652	78
1869	867	1,272	147	656	76
1870	936	1,368	146	721	77
1871	1,015	1,521	150		
1872	1,072	1,732	162		
1873	1,149	1,781	155		
1874	1,126	1,631	145		
1875	1,113	1,533	138		
1876	1,099	1,370	125		
1877	1,089	1,367	126		
1878	1,059	1,277	120		
1879	1,032	1,261	122		
1880	1,076	1,310	122		
1881	1,117	1,345	120		
1882	1,160	1,350	116		
1883	1,153	1,334	116		
1884	1,124	1,251	111		
1885	1,115	1,170	105		
1886	1,136	1,148	101		
1887	1,185	1,184	100		
1888	1,259	1,255	100		
1889	1,350	1,330	99		
1890	1,385	1,351	98		
1891	1,373	1,276	93		
1892	1,335	1,190	89		
1893	1,339	1,158	86	516	39
1894	1,418	1,121	79	490	35
1895	1,447	1,204	83	505	35

Table 18 (continued)

Years	Net national income (a) (current prices)	Total bills drawn (b)	(b)/(a) × 100 (c)	Inland bills drawn (d)	(d)/(a) × 100 (e)
1896	1,484	1,197	81	510	34
1897	1,538	1,183	77	517	34
1898	1,618	1,194	74	505	31
1899	1,700	1,260	74	516	30
1900	1,750	1,240	71	507	29
1901	1,727	1,255	73	499	29
1902	1,740	1,252	72	512	29
1903	1,717	1,235	72	501	29
1904	1,704	1,254	74	510	30
1905	1,776	1,384	78	538	30
1906	1,874	1,480	79	562	30
1907	1,966	1,551	79	586	30
1908	1,875	1,412	75	529	28
1909	1,907	1,469	77	543	28
1910	1,984	1,548	78	571	29
1911	2,076	1,605	77	585	28
1912	2,181	1,732	79	609	28
1913	2,265	1,854	82	651	29

* For net national income, calendar years.
SOURCE: Mitchell & Deane, *Abstract of British Historical Statistics*, pp. 367–8.

Table 19. *Unlapsed currency of bills held by Parr's Bank and Liverpool Union Bank*

	Liverpool Union Bank				Parr's Bank			
End of years	Bills discounted £	Rebate on bills discounted £	Rate of discount %	Days of unlapsed currency	Bills discounted £	Rebate on bills discounted £	Rate of discount %	Days of unlapsed currency
1864	1,700,836	16,192	6	57·9				
1865	1,841,780	19,647	7	55·6				
1866	1,595,861	13,668	5	62·5	379,390	2,554	5	49·1
1867	1,522,055	12,130	5	58·2	392,801	2,773	5	51·5
1868	1,427,466	11,102	5	56·8	401,557	4,167	5	75·8
1869	1,739,990	12,578	5	52·8	462,118	3,465	5	54·7
1870	1,646,166	12,021	5	53·3	450,788	2,967	5	48·0
1871	1,920,897	14,326	5	54·4	450,890	2,821	5	45·7
1872	2,206,090	15,862	5	52·5	561,545	3,693	5	47·9
1873	2,346,596	16,146	5	50·2	712,770	4,127	5	42·3
1874	1,727,460	14,799	6	52·1	694,690	4,818	6	42·2
1875	1,644,702	13,927	5	61·8	646,252	4,477	5	50·6
1876	1,250,714	9,629	5	56·2	527,085	3,538	5	49·0
1877	1,677,289				575,364	3,921	5	49·7
1878	1,595,455	11,769	5	53·8	659,092	4,202	5	46·5
1879	1,898,860	12,851	5	49·4	647,196	4,363	5	49·2
1880	1,600,916	9,636	5	43·9	725,721	4,651	5	46·8
1881	1,541,583	10,225	5	48·4	572,681	3,281	(5)*	(41·8)
1882	1,633,309	11,284	5	50·4	571,262	3,270	5	41·8
1883	1,873,479	13,493	5	52·6	1,037,272	6,122	5	43·1
1884	1,349,718	8,400	5	45·4	717,502	4,237	5	43·1
1885	1,388,170	8,985	5	47·2	806,138	4,177	5	37·8
1886	1,197,013	8,221	5	50·1	640,042	3,409	5	38·9
1887	1,034,506	6,686	5	47·2	874,088	6,576	5	54·9
1888	1,215,652	9,021	5	54·2	554,569	2,906	5	38·2
1889	1,305,055	12,268	6	57·2	745,474	5,396	6	44·0
1890	1,614,680	11,787	5	53·3	676,901	3,982	5	42·9
1891	1,608,991	12,847	5	58·3	903,046	5,692	5	46·0
1892	2,006,547	14,358	5	52·2	1,484,538	10,411	5	51·2
1893	1,497,207	10,543	5	51·4	1,334,393	8,878	5	48·6
1894	1,270,058	9,024	5	51·9	1,338,600	10,034	5	54·7
1895	1,437,659	9,586	5	48·7	1,697,150	11,340	5	48·8
1896	1,347,086	10,360	5	56·1	2,142,727	14,679	5	50·0
1897	1,023,787	7,366	5	52·5	2,316,571	15,693	5	49·5
1898	1,175,734	10,044	5	62·4	2,093,317	14,713	5	51·3
1899	1,060,240	8,789	6	50·4	2,199,917	16,684	6	46·1
1900					2,279,878	13,713	5	43·9
1901					2,421,818	13,844	5	41·7
1902					2,460,629	17,194	5	51·0
1903					2,689,705	14,143	5	38·4
1904					2,384,713	14,641	5	44·8
1905					2,432,197	15,096	5	45·3
1906					2,919,075	22,088	6	46·0
1907					2,557,888	24,173	7	49·3
1908					2,243,180	14,200	5	46·2

* Provisional figures given by author: no figure given by *The Economist*.
SOURCE: *The Economist*, Banking Supplement.

Table 20. Nine-year moving average of unlapsed currency of bills held by Liverpool Union Bank and Parr's Bank

(figures are in days)

End of years	Liverpool Union Bank	Parr's Bank	End of years	Liverpool Union Bank	Parr's Bank
1868	56·0		1888	51·7	44·1
1869	55·1		1889	52·3	44·7
1870	54·8	50·8	1890	52·9	46·6
1871	54·7	51·0	1891	52·7	47·7
1872	54·5	50·7	1892	53·7	47·2
1873	54·2	47·8	1893	53·5	48·4
1874	54·3	46·9	1894	54·1	49·2
1875	53·8	47·0	1895	53·8	49·6
1876	52·5	47·1	1896		49·3
1877	52·0	46·5	1897		48·3
1878	52·0	46·4	1898		48·5
1879	52·1	46·5	1899		46·7
1880	50·0	46·6	1900		46·3
1881	48·9	45·2	1901		45·8
1882	49·0	44·1	1902		45·4
1883	48·3	44·6	1903		45·2
1884	48·8	43·7	1904		45·2
1885	50·3	43·1			
1886	50·8	42·7			
1887	51·7	43·2			

Table 21. Re-discounted bills and other items of balance-sheets of Liverpool Commercial Banking Co. and North-Western Bank

(figures are in £ thousands)

Dates	Liverpool Commercial Banking Co.					North-Western Bank				
	Deposits	Cash on hand and at bankers	Loans	Bills	Bills re-discounted and foreign bills sold	Deposits	Cash on hand and at call	Discounts and loans	Bills in circulation	Acceptances, credits, drafts, etc.
1861.12.31	605	113	*277	735	0					
1862.8.1										
1862.12.31	622	126	*312	690	14					
1863.8.1										
1863.12.31	612	135	*392	662	0					
1864.8.1	819	175	*396	819	not stated					
1864.12.31	633	126	*459	522	471	722	70	925	427	51
1865.8.1	657	116	*440	595	not stated					
1865.12.31	758	135	*460	742	260	1,010	91	1,341	899	637
1866.8.1	636	87	*391	596	426					
1866.12.31	622	121	*418	685	169	744	74	1,683	297	177
1867.8.1	723	226	*464	568	285					
1867.12.31	774	130	*446	648	0	565	106	848	137	67
1868.8.1										
1868.12.31	846	411	*279	584	16	639	81	965	217	154
1869.8.1	664	140	*401	655	138					
1869.12.31	665	199	*424	605	62	648	99	977	257	128
1870.8.1	746	206	*309	667	6					
1870.12.31	753	46	*418	727	109	602	114	928	51	62
1871.7.31	1,046	259	*426	766	90					
1871.12.31	864	58	*468	856	136	758	97	1,114	291	45
1872.7.31										
1872.12.31	1,089	101	*455	1,014	5	792	166	1,094	92	85
1873.7.31	1,127	126	*698	840	†393					

Table 21 (continued)

(figures are in £ thousands)

Dates	Liverpool Commercial Banking Co.					North-Western Bank				
	Deposits	Cash on hand and at bankers	Loans	Bills	Bills re-discounted and foreign bills sold	Deposits	Cash on hand and at call	Discounts and loans	Bills in circulation	Acceptances, credits, drafts, etc.
1873.12.31	1,235	88	*704	930		934	120	1,298	215	131
1874.6.30										
1874.12.31	980	124	*689	652		1,102	141	1,457	132	98
1875.6.30	1,224	371	338	918						
1875.12.31						891	115	1,283	481	225
1876.6.30										
1876.12.31	1,167	642	264	663		830	122	1,213	321	
1877.6.30	1,132	246	671	620						
1877.12.31	975	377	365	636		900	117	1,299	306	
1878.6.30	944	122	647	582						
1878.12.31	806	266	583	551		740	115	1,119	345	
1879.6.30	828	235	584	416						
1879.12.31	916	355	456	511		847	125	1,218	446	
1880.6.30	1,018	265	556	602						
1880.12.31	1,015	498	437	484		805	122	1,188	484	
1881.6.30	904	211	496	610						
1881.12.31	1,012	355	227	833		883	105	1,295	425	
1882.6.30										
1882.12.31	933	203	508	621		1,002	129	1,400	779	
1883.6.30										
1883.12.31	940	243	595	502		920	111	1,336	538	

* May contain acceptances.

† After 31 July 1873, the amount of re-discounted bills is not disclosed.

SOURCE: *The Economist* Banking Supplements.

Table 22. *Assets and liabilities of banks in Liverpool (main items), 1864–83*

(figures are in £ thousands)

Dates	Adelphi Bank			Liverpool Union Bank				National Bank of Liverpool		
	Deposits	Loans and discounts (includes other securities)	Cash on hand and at call	Deposits	Bills	Loans	Cash on hand and at call	Deposits (includes bills on London)	Loans and discounts	Cash on hand and at bankers
1864.12.31	164	251	27	1,806	1,700	339	305	1,072	1,264	124
1865.6.30	188	300	20					738	1,010	120
1865.12.31	238	347	27	1,787	1,842	270	270	1,598	1,853	159
1866.6.30	212	337	14					881	1,293	159
1866.12.31	226	338	24	1,530	1,596	318	219			
1867.6.30	235	347	26							
1867.12.31	219	328	28	1,480	1,522	243	332	693	1,067	133
1868.6.30	209	313	33							
1868.12.31	224	301	41	1,603	1,427	127	677	945	1,305	161
1869.6.30	215	302	34							
1869.12.31				1,649	1,740	228	309	757	1,159	123
1870.6.30	226	338	30					652	1,050	124
1870.12.31	186	299	30	1,507	1,646	257	256	*295	712	82
1871.6.30	241	314	38					813	1,062	187
1871.12.31				2,060	1,921	249	557	877	1,007	309
1872.6.30	200	263	32					910	1,142	212
1872.12.31	184	218	36	2,628	2,206	246	872	831	1,010	273
1873.6.30	186	227	35					828	1,113	170
1873.12.31	179	258	31	2,879	2,347	317	930	721	877	366
1874.6.30	204	280	36					649	1,053	119

Table 22 (continued)

(figures are in £ thousands)

Dates	Adelphi Bank			Liverpool Union Bank				National Bank of Liverpool		
	Deposits	Loans and discounts (includes other securities)	Cash on hand and at call	Deposits	Bills	Loans	Cash on hand and at call	Deposits (includes bills on London)	Loans and discounts	Cash on hand and at bankers
1874.12.31	189	268	34	2,557	1,727	446	1,126	601	1,031	108
1875.6.30	252	327	43					727	1,173	104
1875.12.31	282	363	42	2,267	1,645	715	681	712	1,124	141
1876.6.30	301	386	41					957	1,408	164
1876.12.31	249	336	41	2,308	1,251	555	1,291	718	1,211	154
1877.6.30								830	1,331	139
1877.12.31	301	380	55	2,242	1,677	563	803	781	1,253	194
1878.6.30								743	1,216	136
1878.12.31	258	340	49	2,107	1,595	556	900	522	938	174
1879.6.30								500	832	258
1879.12.31	277	360	48	2,355	1,899	588	845	647	949	126
1880.6.30								538	917	104
1880.12.31	339	419	55	2,411	1,601	733	1,065	729	1,030	122
1881.6.30								776	1,104	115
1881.12.31	428	526	43	2,405	1,542	1,129	749	643	947	129
1882.6.30								752	1,062	118
1882.12.31	481	576	53	2,579	1,633	1,060	906	Absorbed by Parr's Banking Co.		
1883.6.30										
1883.12.31	495	594	52	2,639	1,873	1,109	699			

* Not a mistake.
SOURCE: *The Economist*, Banking Supplements.

Table 23. Acceptances of banks in England and Wales, 1870–80

(figures in £ thousands)

Years (Dec. 31)	1870	1871	1872	1873	1874	1875	1876	1877	1878	1879	1880
London											
Alliance Bank	253	321	594	611	532	642	727	806	618	531	503
City Bank	1,838	2,327	3,101	3,288	3,261	3,151	3,732	3,182	3,267	2,215	2,299
Consolidated Bank	155	222	179	324	246	221	194	151	182	272	167
Imperial Bank	190	335	480	753	1,068	541	386	293	399	330	355
London & County Bkg. Co.	3,110	2,778	4,244	4,070	2,780	2,162	3,048	2,306	3,301	2,553	2,090
London & Westminster Bank	883	1,016	1,273	1,081	1,038	1,236	929	1,035	719	883	648
National Provincial Bank of England	691	183	595	547	1,043	603	700	661	840	574	437
Union Bank of London	4,205	4,364	5,867	5,464	4,957	4,176	5,315	3,406	4,743	4,093	3,520
London & South-Western Bank	26*	44	41	36	1	4	4	4	2	7	2
Total	11,351	11,590	16,374	16,174	14,926	12,736	15,035	11,844	14,071	11,458	10,021
Cotton districts											
Liverpool Union Bank	258	470	598	601	774	156	112	282	339	386	265
National Bank of Liverpool	27	53	68	41	40	48	91	104	52	47	34
North-Western Bank*	62	45	85	131	98	225	321	306	345	446	484
Parr's Banking Co.†	29	28	30	66	52	37	26	30	31	54	45
Union Bank of Manchester†	18	51	26	47	67	60	106	63	65	42	73
Total	394	647	807	886	1,031	526	656	785	832	975	901
Woollen and worsted districts											
Bank of Leeds†	159	115	146	58	75	111	75	Absorbed by National Provincial Bank			
Other English and Welsh counties											
North & South Wales Bank	109*	80*	87*	108*	59	140	143	89	99	51	19
Grand total	12,013	12,432	17,414	17,226	16,091	13,513	15,909	12,718	15,002	12,484	10,941

* At 30 June. † Includes drafts, etc.
SOURCE: *The Economist*, Banking Supplement.

Table 24. Advances plus discounts/deposits ratios of Joint Stock Banks in England and Wales, 1870–80

(figures in £ thousands)

Years (Dec. 31)	1870	1871	1872	1873	1874	1875	1876	1877	1878	1879	1880
London											
Liability to the public (a)	103,980	117,804	132,927	139,789	143,136	141,947	144,425	140,139	139,847	138,938	139,503
Acceptances (b)	11,351	11,590	16,374	16,174	14,926	12,736	15,035	11,844	14,071	11,458	10,021
(a) − (b) (c)	92,629	106,214	116,553	123,615	128,210	129,211	129,390	128,295	116,776	127,480	129,482
Advances and discounts (d)	84,144	92,684	105,835	111,474	113,035	111,124	111,892	106,685	99,373	100,907	101,437
(d) − (b) (e)	72,793	81,094	89,461	95,300	98,109	98,388	96,857	94,841	85,302	89,449	91,416
(e)/(c) × 100 (f)	78·6	76·3	76·8	77·1	76·5	76·1	74·9	73·9	73·0	70·2	70·6
Cotton districts											
Liability to the public (a)	15,839	18,346	21,886	23,940	27,787	28,172	27,269	26,248	24,292	25,700	27,417
Acceptances (b)	394	647	807	886	1,031	526	656	785	832	975	901
(a) − (b) (c)	15,445	17,699	21,079	23,054	26,756	27,646	26,613	25,463	23,460	24,725	26,516
Advances and discounts (d)	16,546	16,856	20,177	20,964	23,761	24,987	23,985	24,127	23,458	23,032	24,827
(d) − (b) (e)	16,152	16,209	19,370	20,078	22,730	24,461	23,329	23,342	22,626	22,057	23,926
(e)/(c) × 100 (f)	104·6	91·6	91·9	87·1	85·0	88·5	87·7	91·7	96·4	89·2	90·2
Woollen and worsted districts											
Liability to the public (a)	6,912	8,188	9,295	9,758	10,781	11,799	12,037	12,100	11,661	10,707	11,424
Acceptances (b)	159	115	146	58	75	111	75	—	—	—	—
(a) − (b) (c)	6,753	8,073	9,149	9,700	10,706	11,688	11,962	12,100	11,661	10,707	11,424
Advances and discounts (d)	9,186	10,558	11,309	12,118	13,497	14,660	15,049	15,012	14,596	13,221	14,171
(d) − (b) (e)	9,027	10,443	11,163	12,060	13,422	14,549	14,974	15,012	14,596	13,221	14,171
(e)/(c) × 100 (f)	133·7	129·4	122·0	124·3	125·4	124·5	125·2	124·1	125·2	123·5	124·0
Northumberland, Durham, Lancs. and Yorks. (excepting cotton and woollen and worsted districts)											
Liability to the public (a)	15,061	18,457	21,094	23,729	24,609	26,349	26,183	26,624	24,288	26,026	27,677
Acceptances (b)	—	—	—	—	—	—	—	—	—	—	—
(a) − (b) (c)	15,061	18,457	21,094	23,729	24,609	26,349	26,183	26,624	24,288	26,026	27,677
Advances and discounts (d)	15,586	17,879	20,346	22,471	22,772	24,407	22,738	24,108	22,889	23,631	24,413
(d) − (b) (e)	15,586	17,879	20,246	22,471	22,772	24,407	22,738	24,108	22,889	23,631	24,413
(e)/(c) × 100 (f)	103·5	96·9	96·0	94·7	92·5	92·6	86·8	90·5	94·2	90·8	88·2

Table 24 (continued)

(figures in £ thousands)

Years (Dec 31)	1870	1871	1872	1873	1874	1875	1876	1877	1878	1879	1880
Derbys., Notts., Staffords., Worcesters. and Warwicks.											
Liability to the public (a)	10,004	11,138	13,357	14,305	16,037	16,547	17,269	16,817	16,810	16,849	17,760
Acceptances (b)	—	—	—	—	—	—	—	—	—	—	—
(a) – (b) (c)	10,004	11,138	13,357	14,305	16,037	16,547	17,269	16,817	16,810	16,849	17,760
Advances and discounts (d)	10,666	11,537	13,149	14,432	15,612	15,475	16,294	16,597	16,773	16,110	16,370
(d) – (b) (e)	10,666	11,537	13,149	14,432	15,612	15,475	16,294	16,597	16,773	16,110	16,370
(e)/(c) × 100 (f)	106·6	103·6	98·4	100·9	97·3	93·5	94·4	98·7	99·8	95·6	92·2
Gloucesters, Monmouth and South Wales											
Liability to the public (a)	5,020	5,366	6,126	6,899	7,453	7,558	7,300	7,416	2,900	3,339	3,510
Acceptances (b)	—	—	—	—	—	—	—	—	—	—	—
(a) – (b) (c)	5,020	5,366	6,126	6,899	7,453	7,558	7,300	7,416	2,900	3,339	3,510
Advances and discounts (d)	4,935	5,195	5,631	6,497	7,100	7,331	7,076	7,245	2,855	3,119	3,315
(d) – (b) (e)	4,935	5,195	5,631	6,497	7,100	7,331	7,076	7,245	2,855	3,119	3,315
(e)/(c) × 100 (f)	98·3	96·8	91·9	94·2	95·3	97·0	96·9	97·7	98·4	93·4	94·4
Other English and Welsh counties											
Liability to the public (a)	12,219	13,463	14,550	15,793	16,875	18,018	18,129	18,633	17,657	17,404	18,253
Acceptances (b)	109	80	87	108	59	140	143	89	99	51	19
(a) – (b) (c)	12,110	13,383	14,463	15,685	16,816	17,878	17,986	18,544	17,558	17,353	18,234
Advances and discounts (d)	9,386	9,765	11,057	11,984	12,289	13,165	13,645	14,198	14,471	12,630	13,039
(d) – (b) (e)	9,277	9,685	10,970	11,876	12,230	13,025	13,502	14,109	14,372	12,579	13,020
(e)/(c) × 100 (f)	76·6	72·4	75·8	75·7	72·7	72·9	75·1	76·1	81·9	72·5	71·4
Total											
Liability to the public (a)	169,035	192,762	219,235	234,213	246,678	250,390	252,612	247,977	228,455	238,963	245,544
Acceptances (b)	12,013	12,432	17,414	17,226	16,091	13,513	15,909	12,718	15,002	12,484	10,941
(a) – (b) (c)	157,022	180,330	201,821	216,987	230,587	236,877	236,703	235,259	213,453	226,479	234,603
Advances and discounts (d)	150,449	164,474	187,404	199,940	208,066	211,149	210,679	207,972	194,415	192,650	197,572
(d) – (b) (e)	138,436	152,042	169,990	182,714	191,975	197,636	194,770	195,254	179,413	180,166	186,631
(e)/(c) × 100 (f)	88·2	84·3	84·2	84·2	83·3	83·4	82·3	83·0	84·1	79·6	79·6

NOTE: Liabilities to the public exclude note issues.
SOURCES: (1) *Miscellaneous Statistics of the U.K.*, BPP, 1882, Vol. 74, pp. 622–7. (2) 'Acceptances' are taken from *The Economist*, Banking Supplements.

Table 25. Advances plus discounts/deposits ratios of banks in England and Wales, 1865–70

Districts*	Years (Dec. 31)	1865	1866	1867	1868	1869	1870
			(figures are in £ thousands)				
London	Deposits (a)			45,535	47,507	48,706	49,592
	Advances and discounts (b)			33,517	35,533	34,935	35,302
	(b)/(a) × 100 (c)			73·6	74·8	71·7	71·2
Cotton districts	Deposits (a)	3,434	3,024	3,244	3,411	3,351	3,318
	Advances and discounts (b)	4,153	3,648	3,735	3,280	3,821	3,809
	(b)/(a) × 100 (c)	120·9	120·6	115·1	96·2	114·0	114·8
Woollen and worsted districts	Deposits (a)	1,080		882	848	909	925
	Advances and discounts (b)	1,420		1,434	1,431	1,497	1,491
	(b)/(a) × 100 (c)	131·5		162·6	168·8	164·7	161·2
Derby., Notts., Staffs., Worcs. and War.	Deposits (a)				3,191	3,365	3,658
	Advances and discounts (b)				3,508	3,786	4,217
	(b)/(a) × 100 (c)				109·9	112·5	115·3
Other English and Welsh counties excluding Northumb., Durham, Lancs., Yorks., Glos., Monmouth and S. Wales	Deposits (a)		3,255	3,355	3,429	3,549	3,596
	Advances and discounts (b)		2,605	2,433	2,311	2,472	2,437
	(b)/(a) × 100 (c)		80·0	72·5	67·4	69·7	67·8
Total	Deposits (a)				58,386	59,880	61,089
	Advances and discounts (b)				46,063	46,511	47,256
	(b)/(a) × 100 (c)				78·9	77·7	77·4

* Districts are arranged so as to conform to the *Miscellaneous Statistics*.

NOTE: No banks in Derbyshire and Nottinghamshire are included in the column titled 'Derby., Notts., Staffs., Worcs. and Warwicks.'.

SOURCE: *The Economist*, Banking Supplements. Figures have been taken from balance-sheets of the following banks:

1. *London*: Union Bank of London, Alliance Bank, Consolidated Bank, City Bank, Imperial Bank, London & County Banking Co., Midland Banking Co., London & South-Western Bank, National Provincial Bank of England, Provincial Banking Corp. (London & Provincial Bank).

2. *Cotton districts*: Liverpool Commercial Banking Co., Liverpool Union Bank, Parr's Banking Co.

3. *Woollen and worsted districts*: Bradford Old Bank, Bank of Leeds.

4. *Derby., Notts., Staffs., Worcs. and War.*: Birmingham Joint Stock Bank, Staffordshire Joint Stock Bank, Worcester City & County Banking Co., Birmingham Town & District Banking Co., Birmingham Banking Co.

5. *Other English and Welsh counties*: Wilts. and Dorset Banking Co., Cumberland Union Banking Co., Bank of Whitehaven.

Table 26. *Advances plus discounts/deposits ratios of banks in England and Wales, 1880–96*

(figures are in £ thousands)

Districts†	Years (Dec. 31)	1880	1881	1882	1883	1884	1885	1886	1887	1888
London	Deposits (a)	106,246	113,233	115,792	117,974	115,190	118,457	125,234	127,330	135,541
	Advances and discounts (b)	69,014	75,349	79,812	81,324	77,771	78,649	81,408	83,558	86,047
	(b)/(a) × 100 (c)	65·0	66·5	68·9	68·9	67·5	66·4	65·0	65·6	63·5
Cotton districts	Deposits (a)	*26,832	33,731	35,388	38,444	36,987	37,909	37,060	39,072	39,890
	Advances and discounts (b)	23,052	27,603	29,657	32,485	31,251	29,756	29,867	31,353	30,998
	(b)/(a) × 100 (c)	85·9	81·8	83·8	84·5	84·5	78·5	80·6	80·2	77·7
Woollen and worsted districts	Deposits (a)	5,319	5,400	5,698	5,997	6,030	6,376	6,283	6,557	6,847
	Advances and discounts (b)	6,000	5,839	5,936	6,295	6,295	6,320	6,462	6,293	6,703
	(b)/(a) × 100 (c)	112·8	108·1	104·2	105·0	104·4	99·1	102·8	96·0	97·9
Northumb., Durham, Lancs. and Yorks., excluding cotton and woollen and worsted districts	Deposits (a)	3,156	3,437	3,684	3,866	3,967	4,004	4,021	4,341	4,551
	Advances and discounts (b)	3,059	3,395	3,610	3,755	3,616	3,489	3,543	3,895	3,962
	(b)/(a) × 100 (c)	96·9	98·8	98·0	97·1	91·2	87·1	88·1	89·7	87·1
Derby., Notts, Staffs., Worcs. and War.	Deposits (a)	17,163	19,027	19,986	20,048	23,654	24,317	24,929	25,669	26,431
	Advances and discounts (b)	15,532	16,715	17,174	16,844	18,775	18,534	18,646	19,298	19,241
	(b)/(a) × 100 (c)	90·5	87·8	85·9	84·0	79·4	76·2	74·8	75·2	72·8
Glos, Monmouth and South Wales	Deposits (a)									
	Advances and discounts (b)									
	(b)/(a) × 100 (c)									
Other English and Welsh counties	Deposits (a)	20,601	21,512	23,028	23,994	24,422	25,214	25,935	26,617	27,747
	Advances and discounts (b)	14,013	14,529	15,093	16,031	15,998	15,846	15,997	16,221	16,763
	(b)/(a) × 100 (c)	68·0	67·5	65·5	66·8	65·5	62·8	61·7	60·9	60·4
Total	Deposits (a)	179,317	196,340	203,576	210,323	210,250	216,277	223,462	229,586	241,007
	Advances and discounts (b)	130,570	143,430	151,282	156,734	153,706	152,594	155,923	160,618	163,714
	(b)/(a) × 100 (c)	72·9	73·1	74·3	74·5	73·1	70·6	69·8	70·0	67·9

Table 26 (continued)

(figures are in £ thousands)

Districts†	Years (Dec. 31)	1889	1890	1891	1892	1893	1894	1895	1896
London	Deposits (a)	147,146	148,583	151,041	143,174	142,792	148,699	162,709	161,306
	Advances and discounts (b)	91,774	90,578	94,047	86,370	86,226	88,167	96,005	94,974
	(b)/(a)×100 (c)	62·4	61·0	62·3	60·3	60·4	59·3	59·0	58·9
Cotton districts	Deposits (a)	42,741	45,983	49,438	53,617	51,593	57,963	61,987	66,817
	Advances and discounts (b)	35,261	37,530	38,914	41,745	40,651	39,819	43,136	48,828
	(b)/(a)×100 (c)	82·5	81·6	78·7	77·9	78·8	68·7	69·6	73·1
Woollen and worsted districts	Deposits (a)	7,415	7,014	7,582	7,489	7,719	8,397	8,995	9,278
	Advances and discounts (b)	7,691	7,460	7,334	7,113	7,668	7,558	7,383	7,424
	(b)/(a)×100 (c)	103·7	106·4	96·7	95·0	99·3	90·2	82·1	80·0
Northumb., Durham, Lancs. and Yorks., excluding cotton and woollen and worsted districts	Deposits (a)	4,845	5,122	5,299	6,057	5,748	6,115	6,439	6,905
	Advances and discounts (b)	3,812	3,938	3,772	4,184	4,439	4,352	4,789	5,563
	(b)/(a)×100 (c)	78·7	76·9	71·2	69·1	77·2	71·2	74·4	80·6
Derby, Notts., Staffs., Worcs. and War.	Deposits (a)	30,772	36,122	40,922	45,466	47,171	52,115	57,323	64,766
	Advances and discounts (b)	22,234	25,616	28,087	30,960	32,721	35,042	37,228	43,213
	(b)/(a)×100 (c)	72·3	70·9	68·7	68·1	69·4	67·2	64·9	66·7
Glos., Monmouth and South Wales	Deposits (a)								
	Advances and discounts (b)								
	(b)/(a)×100 (c)								
Other English and Welsh counties	Deposits (a)	30,000	30,121	32,098	31,526	31,085	31,736	33,706	33,897
	Advances and discounts (b)	18,069	18,342	19,598	18,630	18,350	17,210	19,457	19,564
	(b)/(a)×100 (c)	60·2	60·9	61·1	59·1	59·0	54·2	57·7	57·7
Total	Deposits (a)	262,919	272,945	286,380	287,329	286,108	305,005	331,159	342,969
	Advances and discounts (b)	178,841	183,464	191,752	189,002	190,055	192,148	207,998	219,566
	(b)/(a)×100 (c)	68·0	67·2	67·0	65·8	66·4	63·0	62·8	64·0

Table 26 (continued)

* Does not include figures for Manchester & Salford Bank.

† Districts are arranged so as to conform to the *Miscellaneous Statistics*. County names in the titles of the columns do not necessarily imply that banks in the counties are included in the figures of the column.

SOURCE: *The Economist*, Banking Supplements. Figures are taken from balance-sheets of the following banks:

1. *London*: London and Westminster Bank, Union Bank of London, Alliance Bank, Central Bank of London, Consolidated Bank, Imperial Bank, City Bank, Capital & Counties Bank, London & County Banking Co, London & South-Western Bank, London & Yorkshire Bank, National Provincial Bank of England.

2. *Cotton districts*: Bank of Liverpool (Martins Bank), Liverpool Commercial Banking Co, Liverpool Union Bank, Manchester & County Bank, Manchester & Liverpool District Banking Co, Manchester & Salford Bank (from 1881) (Williams Deacon's Bank), Parr's Banking Co, Preston Banking Co.

3. *Woollen and worsted districts*: Huddersfield Banking Co, Bradford Old Bank, Craven Bank.

4. *Northumb., Durham, Lancs, and Yorks.* (excepting cotton and woollen and worsted districts): North-Eastern Banking Co., Sheffield Banking Co., Sheffield & Rotherham Joint Stock Bank.

5. *Derby, Notts., Staffs., Worcs. and War. (Black Country)*: Birmingham & Midland Bank, Birmingham Banking Co. (Metropolitan Bank), Birmingham, Dudley & District Banking Co. (United Counties Bank), Birmingham Joint Stock Bank, Lloyds Banking Co., Staffordshire Joint Stock Bank, Crompton & Evan's Union Bank, Nottingham Joint Stock Bank, Worcester City & County Banking Co.

6. *Other English and Welsh counties*: Devon & Cornwall Banking Co., Stuckey's Banking Co., Wilts. & Dorset Banking Co., Bucks. & Oxon Union Bank, Stamford, Spalding & Boston Banking Co., Bank of Whitehaven, Carlisle City & District Banking Co., Cumberland Union Banking Co., Bristol & West of England Bank, Leicestershire Banking Co, North & South Wales Bank.

Table 27. Advances plus discounts/deposits ratios of banks in England and Wales, 1897–1913

(figures are in £ thousands)

Year ended Dec. 31		1897	1898	1899	1900	1901	1902	1903	1904	1905
London Banks	Deposits (a)	253,603	266,917	275,988	305,142	304,962	319,946	330,627	338,638	349,596
	Advances and discounts (b)	154,086	158,855	167,751	183,863	183,748	189,194	206,440	205,729	210,981
	(b)/(a) × 100 (c)	60·9	59·5	60·8	60·3	60·2	59·1	62·4	60·8	60·4
Banks in cotton districts	Deposits (a)	49,429	51,180	53,684	50,119	48,465	48,864	45,940	46,762	48,654
	Advances and discounts (b)	36,570	38,337	39,936	37,870	34,672	35,703	34,215	34,540	34,661
	(b)/(a) × 100 (c)	74·0	74·9	74·4	75·6	71·5	73·1	74·5	73·9	71·2
Banks in Derby., Notts., Black Country, Yorks. and Newcastle-upon-Tyne	Deposits (a)	23,284	23,522	25,351	26,978	26,657	26,274	25,495	27,250	26,241
	Advances and discounts (b)	18,417	19,291	20,616	20,947	20,884	20,374	20,337	20,602	19,450
	(b)/(a) × 100 (c)	79·1	82·0	81·3	77·7	78·3	77·5	79·8	75·6	74·1
Banks in other districts of England and Wales	Deposits (a)	37,061	38,209	39,374	36,504	36,229	35,809	35,154	35,528	36,126
	Advances and discounts (b)	21,873	23,015	24,017	20,975	20,527	20,752	21,389	21,036	21,189
	(b)/(a) × 100 (c)	59·0	60·2	61·0	57·5	56·7	57·9	60·9	59·2	58·6
Total	Deposits (a)	362,377	379,828	394,397	418,743	416,313	430,893	437,216	448,178	460,617
	Advances and discounts (b)	230,946	239,498	252,320	263,655	259,831	266,023	282,381	281,907	286,281
	(b)/(a) × 100 (c)	63·7	63·1	64·0	63·0	62·4	61·7	64·6	62·9	62·2

Table 27 (continued)

(figures are in £ thousands)

Year ended Dec. 31	...	1906	1907	1908	1909	1910	1911	1912	1913
London Banks									
Deposits (a)		365,580	367,104	397,879	411,825	435,983	451,375	471,532	495,080
Advances and discounts (b)		225,142	229,348	238,467	244,596	270,230	282,709	304,656	319,716
(b)/(a) × 100 (c)		61·6	62·5	59·9	59·4	62·0	62·6	64·6	64·6
Banks in cotton districts									
Deposits (a)		52,322	60,080	61,378	61,672	62,822	65,493	70,713	72,766
Advances and discounts (b)		38,922	44,840	44,558	43,158	44,541	45,059	48,437	50,131
(b)/(a) × 100 (c)		74·4	74·6	72·6	70·0	70·9	68·8	68·5	68·9
Banks in Derby., Notts., Black Country, Yorks. and Newcastle-upon-Tyne									
Deposits (a)		22,250	22,721	23,947	24,280	25,385	26,185	27,710	29,348
Advances and discounts (b)		16,643	16,906	17,426	17,477	17,928	19,091	20,080	20,860
(b)/(a) × 100 (c)		74·8	74·4	72·8	72·0	70·6	72·9	72·5	71·1
Banks in other districts of England and Wales									
Deposits (a)		32,379	32,499	22,135	15,971	16,472	12,887	13,111	13,311
Advances and discounts (b)		19,205	19,586	12,119	10,111	10,587	7,977	8,307	8,531
(b)/(a) × 100 (c)		59·3	60·3	54·7	63·3	64·3	61·9	63·4	64·1
Total									
Deposits (a)		472,531	482,404	505,339	513,748	540,662	555,940	583,066	610,505
Advances and discounts (b)		299,912	310,680	312,570	315,342	343,286	354,836	381,480	399,238
(b)/(a) × 100 (c)		63·5	64·4	61·8	61·4	63·5	63·8	65·4	65·4

SOURCE: *The Economist*, Banking Supplements. Figures are taken from balance-sheets of the following banks:

1. *London*: London & Westminster Bank, Union Bank of London, City Bank, Capital & Counties Bank, London & County Banking Co., London & South-Western Bank, London & Yorkshire Bank, National Provincial Bank of England, London & Midland Bank, Metropolitan Bank, Lloyds Bank, Parr's Bank.

2. *Cotton districts*: Bank of Liverpool (Martins Bank), Liverpool Union Bank, Manchester & County Bank, Manchester & Liverpool District Banking Co., Williams Deacon's and Manchester & Salford Bank.

3. *Derby., Notts., Black County, Yorks. and Newcastle-upon-Tyne*: Bradford Old Bank, Craven Bank, North-Eastern Banking Co., Sheffield Banking Co., Sheffield & Rotherham Joint Stock Bank, Birmingham District & Counties Banking Co. (United Counties Bank), Crompton & Evan's Union Bank, Nottingham Joint Stock Bank.

4. *Other districts of England and Wales*: Bank of Whitehaven, Cumberland Union Banking Co., Leicestershire Banking Co., North & South Wales Bank, Bucks. & Oxon Union Bank, Devon & Cornwall Banking Co., Stuckey's Banking Co., Stamford, Spalding & Boston Banking Co., Wilts. & Dorset Banking Co.

Table 28. Market rates of discount of three months' bank bills, 1855–1913
(averages of financial years)

Years	Market rates of discount of three months' bank bills %	Years	Market rates of discount of three months' bank bills %	Years	Market rates of discount of three months' bank bills %
1855	4·74	1875	2·94	1895	0·81
1856	5·48	1876	1·36	1896	1·78
1857	5·78	1877	2·46	1897	1·99
1858	2·43	1878	3·42	1898	2·52
1859	2·97	1879	1·66	1899	3·67
1860	4·99	1880	2·41	1900	3·74
1861	3·80	1881	3·23	1901	2·97
1862	2·85	1882	3·11	1902	3·14
1863	5·09	1883	2·96	1903	3·32
1864	6·80	1884	2·58	1904	2·52
1865	5·37	1885	1·71	1905	2·93
1866	5·56	1886	2·42	1906	4·33
1867	1·92	1887	2·07	1907	4·13
1868	2·16	1888	2·62	1908	1·95
1869	3·09	1889	3·01	1909	2·40
1870	2·95	1890	3·37	1910	3·25
1871	2·70	1891	2·41	1911	3·02
1872	4·11	1892	1·39	1912	3·94
1873	4·41	1893	2·22	1913	3·81
1874	3·42	1894	0·84		

SOURCE: *The Economist* (weekly figures).

Table 29. Rates of interest in Paris, New York and Berlin and their
differentials from London market rates of discount,* 1861–1913

	Paris market rates (1)	New York call rates (2)	Berlin market rates (3)	(% figures) $\frac{(1)+(2)+(3)}{3}$ (4)	London market rates (5)	(5)−(4) (6)	(5)−(1) (7)
Years							
1861	4·48				3·80		−0·68
1862	3·61				2·85		−0·76
1863	4·84				5·09		+0·25
1864	5·66				6·80		+1·14
1865	3·70				5·37		+1·67
1866	3·02				5·56		+2·54
1867	2·20				1·92		−0·28
1868	1·56				2·16		+0·60
1869	2·12				3·09		+0·97
1870	4·23				2·95		−1·28
1871	5·09				2·70		−2·39
1872	4·79				4·11		−0·68
1873	4·86				4·41		−0·45
1874	3·59				3·42		−0·17
1875	3·11				2·94		−0·17
1876	1·85				1·36		−0·49
1877	1·69				2·46		+0·77
1878	2·14				3·42		+1·28
1879	2·15				1·66		−0·49
1880	2·69				2·41		−0·28
1881	3·89	3·45	3·87	3·74	3·23	−0·51	−0·66
1882	3·13	3·11	3·71	3·32	3·11	−0·21	−0·02
1883	2·59	2·08	2·99	2·55	2·96	+0·41	+0·37
1884	2·54	1·77	3·00	2·44	2·58	+0·14	+0·04
1885	2·37	1·39	2·65	2·14	1·71	−0·43	−0·66
1886	2·21	3·21	2·39	2·60	2·42	−0·18	+0·21
1887	2·39	3·76	2·02	2·72	2·07	−0·65	−0·32
1888	2·85	1·93	2·22	2·33	2·62	+0·29	−0·23
1889	2·48	3·78	3·11	3·12	3·01	−0·11	+0·53
1890	2·63	3·43	3·60	3·22	3·37	+0·15	+0·74
1891	2·44	2·57	2·76	2·59	2·41	−0·18	−0·03
1892	1·78	2·86	1·79	2·14	1·39	−0·75	−0·39
1893	2·26	2·54	3·28	2·69	2·22	−0·47	−0·04
1894	1·65	1·14	1·59	1·46	0·84	−0·62	−0·81
1895	1·64	2·11	2·26	2·00	0·81	−1·19	−0·83
1896	1·78	2·64	3·19	2·54	1·78	−0·76	0·00
1897	1·86	1·68	3·04	2·19	1·99	−0·20	+0·13
1898	2·30	2·16	3·88	2·78	2·52	−0·26	+0·22
1899	3·09	3·30	4·58	3·66	3·67	+0·01	+0·58
1900	2·92	2·37	4·12	3·14	3·74	+0·60	+0·82
1901	2·36	4·30	2·76	3·14	2·97	−0·17	+0·61
1902	2·46	4·43	2·35	3·08	3·14	+0·06	+0·68
1903	2·69	2·74	3·17	2·87	3·32	+0·45	+0·63
1904	2·04	1·86	2·95	2·28	2·52	+0·24	+0·48
1905	2·25	3·90	3·18	3·11	2·93	−0·18	+0·68
1906	2·79	4·89	4·35	4·01	4·33	+0·32	+1·54
1907	3·28	3·62	5·01	3·97	4·13	+0·16	+0·85
1908	1·84	1·74	2·96	2·18	1·95	−0·23	+0·11
1909	1·94	2·77	3·07	2·59	2·40	−0·19	+0·46
1910	2·38	2·64	3·62	2·88	3·25	+0·37	+0·87
1911	2·81	2·48	3·66	2·98	3·02	+0·04	+0·21
1912	3·31	3·77	4·57	3·88	3·94	+0·06	+0·63
1913	3·59	2·86	4·43	3·63	3·81	+0·18	+0·22

* The rates are those for the discount of three months' bank bills, except for New York rates.
SOURCE: *The Economist*.

Table 30. Rates of interest (monthly averages)

Years	Months	Day-to-day money	3 Months bank bills	6 Months bank bills	Bank rate	Paris market rate	New York call rate	Berlin market rate
				(% figures)				
1855	Jan.	4·00	4·74		5·00			
	Feb.	4·00	4·75		5·00			
	Mar.	4·00	4·50		5·00			
	Apr.	3·50	3·69		4·50			
	May	2·75	3·28		4·00			
	Jun.	2·50	3·09		3·63			
	Jul.	2·50	2·91		3·50			
	Aug.	2·90	3·25		3·50			
	Sept.	4·38	4·46		4·50			
	Oct.	4·75	5·50		6·40			
	Nov.	4·33	6·67		7·00			
	Dec.		6·00		7·00			
1856	Jan.		6·00		7·00			
	Feb.		6·00		7·00			
	Mar.	*7·25	6·00		7·00			
	Apr.		6·00		7·00			
	May	4·83	5·53		6·40			
	Jun.	3·83	4·54		4·88			
	Jul.	3·54	3·78		4·50			
	Aug.	3·85	4·30		4·50			
	Sept.		4·38		4·50			
	Oct.	5·00	6·67		6·60			
	Nov.	†5·38	6·75		7·00			
	Dec.		6·00		6·25			
1857	Jan.		5·90		6·00			
	Feb.	††*6·50	5·92		6·00			
	Mar.		6·00		6·00			
	Apr.	*7·50	6·56		6·50			
	May	7·75	6·50		6·50			
	Jun.	*6·50	6·16		6·25			
	Jul.	*5·50	5·52		5·70			
	Aug.	*3·75	5·42		5·50			
	Sept.	*4·25	5·50		5·50			
	Oct.	*5·00	6·87		6·90			
	Nov.		*9·00		9·75			
	Dec.		8·66		9·50			
1858	Jan.	2·87	4·35		5·60			
	Feb.	*2·50	2·46		3·13			
	Mar.		2·37		3·00			
	Apr.	*2·25	2·45	3·37	3·00			
	May	*2·25	2·37	3·75	3·00			
	Jun.		2·59	*3·75	3·00			
	Jul.		2·60	*4·00	3·00			
	Aug.		2·47	4·00	3·00			
	Sept.		2·54	*4·25	3·00			
	Oct.	*1·00	2·29		3·00			
	Nov.	2·12	2·42	3·70	3·00			
	Dec.		2·45		2·60			

* One observation only.
† Up to Dec. 1856, rate for floating money.
‡ From Feb. 1857, rate for short loans on Government securities.

Table 30 (continued)

Years	Months	Day-to-day money	3 Months bank bills	6 Months bank bills	Bank rate	Paris market rate	New York call rate	Berlin market rate
				(% figures)				
1859	Jan.	*1·25	2·36		2·50			
	Feb.	*1·00	2·16		2·50			
	Mar.	*1·25	2·44		2·50			
	Apr.		2·80	*4·75	2·70			
	May		4·25		4·50			
	Jun.		2·56		3·13			
	Jul.		2·50		2·70			
	Aug.		2·44		2·50			
	Sept.	*2·25	2·45		2·50			
	Oct.	1·87	2·42		2·50			
	Nov.	*2·00	2·52		2·50			
	Dec.	*2·75	2·48		2·50			
1860	Jan.		2·86	*4·00	2·75			
	Feb.	*1·75	3·97	*5·50	4·00			
	Mar.	3·38	4·35	*4·87	4·10			
	Apr.		4·84	5·93	4·88			
	May	3·91	4·32	*4·75	4·50			
	Jun.	4·12	4·10	5·12	4·00			
	Jul.	2·75	3·97		4·00	3·08		
	Aug.	2·35	3·95	5·18	4·00	3·06		
	Sept.	2·47	3·68		4·00	3·00		
	Oct.	3·00	3·83		4·00	3·00		
	Nov.	2·56	4·67	5·80	5·10	3·75		
	Dec.	4·19	4·90		5·00	*4·00		
1861	Jan.	5·59	6·69		6·75	5·54		
	Feb.	7·19	7·47		7·50	4·79		
	Mar.	6·40	7·40		7·60	4·60		
	Apr.	3·68	4·91		5·20	4·50		
	May	4·55	5·42	*6·00	5·60	4·50		
	Jun.	5·66	6·00		6·00	4·50		
	Jul.	4·50	5·62		6·00	4·50		
	Aug.	3·55	4·36		4·60	4·20		
	Sept.	2·69	3·31		3·75	4·59		
	Oct.	2·38	3·04		3·50	5·75		
	Nov.	1·65	2·69	3·65	3·10	4·90		
	Dec.	1·87	2·84	3·56	3·00	4·25		
1862	Jan.	1·50	2·45	3·08	2·60	4·15		
	Feb.	1·63	2·53	3·44	2·50	4·00		
	Mar.	1·94	2·41	3·00	2·50	3·88		
	Apr.	1·38	2·36	3·00	2·50	3·25		
	May	1·45	2·76	3·58	2·70	3·00		
	Jun.	2·00	2·84	3·88	3·00	3·34		
	Jul.	1·88	2·14	3·25	2·50	3·13		
	Aug.	1·38	1·92	3·00	2·00	3·15		
	Sept.	1·44	2·03	2·94	2·00	3·22		
	Oct.	1·69	2·20	2·95	2·20	3·35		
	Nov.	1·67	2·94	3·59	3·00	3·78		
	Dec.	2·00	3·00	3·72	3·00	3·69		

* One observation only.

Table 30 (continued)

		Day-to-day money	3 Months bank bills	(% figures) 6 Months bank bills	Bank rate	Paris market rate	New York call rate	Berlin market rate
Years	Months							
1863	Jan.	2·80	3·79	4·55	3·80	4·55		
	Feb.	3·13	4·22	5·00	4·50	4·63		
	Mar.	3·75	4·00	4·53	4·00	4·17		
	Apr.	3·00	3·56	4·09	3·88	3·84		
	May	2·50	3·50	4·18	3·40	3·85		
	Jun.	3·13	4·00	4·59	4·00	3·69		
	Jul.	2·63	3·95	4·43	4·00	3·80		
	Aug.	2·25	3·97	4·34	4·00	3·84		
	Sept.	3·19	4·00	4·31	4·00	3·56		
	Oct.	3·10	4·03	4·43	4·00	4·54		
	Nov.	4·63	6·05	6·50	6·00	6·06		
	Dec.	5·25	7·78	7·67	7·75	6·63		
1864	Jan.	6·10	7·36	7·33	7·40	7·00		
	Feb.	5·00	6·97	7·38	7·00	6·31		
	Mar.	4·63	5·89	6·03	6·00	6·00		
	Apr.	5·15	6·50	6·97	6·40	6·00		
	May	6·19	8·08	8·25	8·25	6·75		
	Jun.	5·81	6·38	6·72	6·50	5·66		
	Jul.	5·75	6·28	6·70	6·20	6·00		
	Aug.	5·88	7·91	8·31	8·00	6·00		
	Sept.	6·25	8·75	8·93	8·80	6·68		
	Oct.	5·25	8·97	9·13	9·00	7·38		
	Nov.	5·06	7·72	7·69	8·00	6·50		
	Dec.	6·10	6·38	6·55	6·40	4·95		
1865	Jan.	4·50	5·39	5·88	5·50	4·50		
	Feb.	4·06	4·84	5·38	5·00	4·06		
	Mar.	4·10	4·40	4·78	4·40	3·45		
	Apr.	3·06	3·92	4·44	4·00	3·41		
	May	2·88	4·38	5·06	4·38	3·50		
	Jun.	3·15	3·23	4·00	3·20	2·85		
	Jul.	2·31	3·25	4·19	3·13	2·97		
	Aug.	2·44	4·00	4·78	4·00	2·94		
	Sept.	3·90	4·08	4·65	4·10	2·87		
	Oct.	4·94	6·72	6·75	6·75	4·56		
	Nov.	5·13	6·97	6·75	6·75	4·38		
	Dec.	5·40	6·25	6·60	6·20	3·85		
1866	Jan.	4·56	7·63	7·63	8·00	4·97		
	Feb.	6·94	7·61	7·42	7·75	4·53		
	Mar.	6·25	6·36	6·50	6·40	3·53		
	Apr.	4·44	5·91	6·00	6·00	3·47		
	May	6·88	9·00	9·00	9·50	4·00		
	Jun.	7·30	9·60	9·40	10·00	3·70		
	Jul.	6·25	9·13	8·88	10·00	3·41		
	Aug.	6·05	7·50	7·10	8·20	2·90		
	Sept.	4·13	4·66	4·44	4·88	2·63		
	Oct.	3·06	4·19	5·88	4·50	3·25		
	Nov.	3·20	3·83	4·35	4·10	2·56		
	Dec.		3·72	4·13	3·75	2·56		

* One observation only.

Table 30 (continued)

Years	Months	Day-to-day money	3 Months bank bills	6 Months bank bills	Bank rate	Paris market rate	New York call rate	Berlin market rate
				(% figures)				
1867	Jan.	1·92	3·05	3·56	3·50	2·63		
	Feb.	1·92	2·72	2·86	3·13	2·63		
	Mar.	2·25	2·79	2·88	3·00	2·46		
	Apr.	*1·00	2·75	2·83	3·00	2·28		
	May	1·56	2·74	3·10	2·90	2·50		
	Jun.	2·44	2·28	2·53	2·50	2·13		
	Jul.	1·63	1·89	2·34	2·38	1·91		
	Aug.	1·50	1·63	2·00	2·00	2·25		
	Sept.	1·25	1·56	1·88	2·00	2·25		
	Oct.	1·13	1·31	1·81	2·00	2·50		
	Nov.	1·06	1·83	1·95	2·00	2·00		
	Dec.	1·56	1·81	2·31	2·00	2·06		
1868	Jan.	1·15	1·70	1·90	2·00	2·25		
	Feb.	1·19	1·59	1·97	2·00	2·25		
	Mar.	1·63	1·92	2·53	2·00	2·03		
	Apr.	1·50	2·00	2·69	2·00	1·94		
	May	1·35	2·08	2·68	2·00	1·89		
	Jun.	1·42	1·61	2·25	2·00	1·38		
	Jul.	1·25	1·55	2·10	2·00	1·38		
	Aug.	1·56	1·83	2·34	2·00	1·72		
	Sept.	*1·00	1·58	2·25	2·00	1·50		
	Oct.		1·51	2·22	2·00	1·44		
	Nov.		2·17	2·88	2·25	1·48		
	Dec.	*2·25	2·88	3·53	3·00	1·50		
1869	Jan.	1·38	2·78	3·30	3·00	1·50		
	Feb.	2·75	2·95	3·47	3·00	1·50		
	Mar.	*2·81	2·97	3·50	3·00	1·50		
	Apr.	3·42	3·80	3·95	4·00	1·50		
	May	3·42	4·58	5·00	4·50	2·13		
	Jun.	3·06	3·73	3·94	4·00	2·13		
	Jul.	2·06	2·74	2·83	3·20	2·13		
	Aug.	1·75	2·38	2·78	2·75	2·13		
	Sept.	1·75	2·34	2·73	2·50	2·31		
	Oct.	1·80	2·39	3·03	2·50	2·10		
	Nov.	2·00	3·08	3·56	3·00	2·25		
	Dec.	2·25	2·99	3·41	3·00	2·25		
1870	Jan.	3·00	2·88	3·13	3·00	2·25		
	Feb.	2·81	3·01	3·19	3·00	2·25		
	Mar.	2·69	3·14	3·13	3·00	2·00		
	Apr.	2·75	3·00	2·99	3·00	2·08		
	May	2·75	3·03	3·14	3·00	2·25		
	Jun.	2·83	2·98	3·13	3·00	2·25		
	Jul.		3·65	3·96	3·88	3·10		
	Aug.	*2·75	4·83	4·86	5·00	6·17		
	Sept.		2·96	3·25	3·10	6·00		
	Oct.	*1·75	2·45	3·09	2·50	6·00		
	Nov.		2·38	3·38	2·50	6·00		
	Dec.	2·25	2·29	3·19	2·50			

* One observation only.

Table 30 (continued)

Years	Months	Day-to-day money	3 Months bank bills	6 Months bank bills	Bank rate	Paris market rate	New York call rate	Berlin market rate
				(% figures)				
1871	Jan.		2·23	3·01	2·50			
	Feb.	*2·00	2·63	3·63	2·50			
	Mar.		2·94	3·95	3·00			
	Apr.		2·33	2·91	2·63			
	May		2·33	2·92	2·50			
	Jun.		2·23	2·91	2·35			
	Jul.		1·78	2·53	2·06			
	Aug.		1·73	2·42	2·00	*5·00		
	Sept.		2·48	3·14	2·60	4·70		
	Oct.		4·33	4·69	4·75	5·00		
	Nov.		3·51	3·91	4·50	5·38		
	Dec.	*4·00	2·98	3·22	3·20	5·50		
1872	Jan.		2·67	2·95	3·00	5·00		
	Feb.		2·98	3·45	3·00	5·42		
	Mar.		2·99	3·53	3·00	4·72		
	Apr.		3·73	4·16	3·88	4·80		
	May		4·33	4·48	4·60	4·84		
	Jun.		3·09	3·31	3·38	4·50		
	Jul.		3·14	3·47	3·25	4·63		
	Aug.		3·31	3·74	3·50	4·38		
	Sept.		3·81	4·17	3·88	4·66		
	Oct.	*5·75	5·50	5·31	5·75	4·75		
	Nov.	6·17	6·34	6·03	6·40	4·95		
	Dec.	4·75	4·95	5·00	5·25	5·00		
1873	Jan.		4·03	4·16	4·30	5·00		
	Feb.		3·47	4·00	3·50	5·00		
	Mar.	*3·25	3·63	4·25	3·63	5·00		
	Apr.	1·92	3·97	4·47	4·00	5·00		
	May	4·00	4·89	4·88	5·10	4·85		
	Jun.	6·25	5·92	5·31	6·25	4·75		
	Jul.		4·34	4·44	4·88	4·69		
	Aug.	*2·25	3·16	3·86	3·30	4·70		
	Sept.	1·92	3·25	4·06	3·25	4·91		
	Oct.	*1·75	5·55	5·00	6·20	5·40		
	Nov.	6·17	7·31	6·09	8·00	5·94		
	Dec.	4·13	4·31	4·28	4·63	4·75		
1874	Jan.	2·50	3·31	3·69	3·80	4·60		
	Feb.	*3·00	3·41	3·89	3·50	4·51		
	Mar.	3·50	3·44	3·88	3·50	4·19		
	Apr.	2·69	3·38	3·89	3·50	4·13		
	May	4·25	3·65	3·81	3·90	4·25		
	Jun.		2·45	2·94	2·75	3·56		
	Jul.	2·00	2·38	3·18	2·60	3·53		
	Aug.	3·33	3·39	3·80	3·63	3·34		
	Sept.	1·75	2·75	3·34	3·00	3·09		
	Oct.	*2·00	3·44	3·98	3·60	3·75		
	Nov.	2·88	3·95	3·84	4·50	3·72		
	Dec.	6·25	5·34	4·81	6·00	3·66		

* One observation only.

Table 30 (*continued*)

Years	Months	Day-to-day money	3 Months bank bills	6 Months bank bills	Bank rate	Paris market rate	New York call rate	Berlin market rate
				(% figures)				
1875	Jan.	3·08	3·80	4·08	4·40	3·73		
	Feb.	2·44	3·16	3·84	3·25	3·28		
	Mar.	3·25	3·39	3·89	3·50	3·03		
	Apr.	2·95	3·24	3·78	3·50	3·25		
	May	3·13	3·36	3·72	3·50	3·13		
	Jun.	3·00	3·39	3·77	3·50	3·00		
	Jul.	1·95	2·60	3·28	3·00	3·05		
	Aug.	1·06	1·72	2·89	2·13	3·06		
	Sept.	1·06	1·73	2·84	2·00	3·05		
	Oct.	1·92	2·83	3·38	3·20	3·11		
	Nov.	1·88	2·78	2·91	3·50	3·45		
	Dec.	2·08	2·78	2·96	3·20	3·58		
1876	Jan.	3·75	3·85	3·78	4·75	3·06		
	Feb.	3·69	3·64	3·50	4·00	2·81		
	Mar.	3·44	3·38	3·35	3·80	2·75		
	Apr.	1·50	1·88	2·44	2·50	2·53		
	May	*1·00	1·50	2·25	2·00	2·19		
	Jun.		1·54	2·23	2·00	1·25		
	Jul.	*0·75	1·22	1·75	2·00	1·50		
	Aug.		1·00	1·75	2·00	1·25		
	Sept.	0·50	0·98	1·70	2·00	1·58		
	Oct.	*1·00	0·91	1·63	2·00	2·25		
	Nov.	*1·50	1·28	2·03	2·00	1·88		
	Dec.		1·49	2·38	2·00	1·95		
1877	Jan.		1·22	2·00	2·00	2·06		
	Feb.	1·08	1·45	2·28	2·00	2·00		
	Mar.		1·84	2·35	2·00	1·80		
	Apr.		1·70	2·25	2·00	1·84		
	May	*2·25	2·73	2·78	3·00	1·75		
	Jun.		2·40	2·46	3·00	1·45		
	Jul.		1·36	1·81	2·13	1·28		
	Aug.		1·85	2·38	2·20	1·65		
	Sept.		2·64	3·20	3·00	1·44		
	Oct.		4·00	3·86	4·75	1·91		
	Nov.		3·48	3·54	4·80	1·83		
	Dec.	*3·50	3·39	3·31	4·00	1·94		
1878	Jan.		2·14	2·50	3·25	1·77		
	Feb.		1·66	2·30	2·00	1·53		
	Mar.		2·15	2·86	2·20	1·88		
	Apr.		2·52	2·66	3·00	1·80		
	May		2·26	2·49	2·90	1·78		
	Jun.	*1·25	2·00	2·17	2·63	1·77		
	Jul.		2·78	2·80	3·50	1·86		
	Aug.	*4·25	4·15	4·28	4·60	1·83		
	Sept.	4·66	4·23	4·13	5·00	1·67		
	Oct.	*5·50	5·20	5·13	5·50	2·34		
	Nov.		4·70	4·54	5·60	2·71		
	Dec.		4·98	4·80	5·00	2·81		

* One observation only.

Table 30 (continued)

Years	Months	Day-to-day money	3 Months bank bills	(% figures) 6 Months bank bills	Bank rate	Paris market rate	New York call rate	Berlin market rate
1879	Jan.	*3·25	3·33	3·43	4·20	2·71		3·49
	Feb.	*2·13	2·80	3·03	3·00	2·25		2·42
	Mar.		2·08	2·36	2·63	2·09		2·16
	Apr.	1·31	1·33	1·83	2·13	2·38		2·16
	May	0·69	1·16	1·84	2·00	2·21		2·06
	Jun.	1·19	1·38	1·88	2·00	1·72		2·22
	Jul.	*0·50	0·92	1·64	2·00	1·62		2·38
	Aug.	*0·63	1·04	1·78	2·00	1·65		2·21
	Sept.	*0·50	1·03	1·83	2·00	1·63		2·81
	Oct.	0·50	1·34	2·20	2·00	2·24		3·83
	Nov.		2·20	2·84	3·00	2·59		4·00
	Dec.	*2·13	2·50	3·00	3·00	2·28		3·31
1880	Jan.	1·63	1·74	2·40	3·00	2·64		3·25
	Feb.	*2·00	2·50	2·94	3·00	2·59		2·19
	Mar.		2·83	2·97	3·00	2·28		2·20
	Apr.	2·44	2·66	2·95	3·00	2·16		2·71
	May	*2·75	2·91	3·09	3·00	2·33		2·78
	Jun.	2·06	2·41	2·61	2·75	2·21		2·88
	Jul.	1·58	1·83	2·19	2·50	2·33		2·79
	Aug.	1·41	2·11	2·59	2·50	2·20		2·50
	Sept.	*1·75	2·27	2·77	2·50	2·22		4·31
	Oct.	1·71	1·95	2·48	2·50	2·75		4·25
	Nov.	1·46	1·98	2·44	2·50	3·23		3·47
	Dec.	*0·50	2·65	2·86	2·90	3·28		3·48
1881	Jan.	3·58	2·70	3·53	3·38	3·16	3·88	3·16
	Feb.	*3·25	2·97	3·14	3·25	3·16	3·88	2·19
	Mar.	*2·50	2·50	2·67	3·00	3·28	3·63	2·25
	Apr.	2·50	2·41	2·61	2·90	3·18	3·80	2·70
	May	*1·75	1·83	2·17	2·50	3·31	2·44	2·88
	Jun.	1·81	1·83	2·09	2·50	3·38	2·69	3·03
	Jul.	*0·88	1·45	1·89	2·50	3·41	2·55	3·28
	Aug.		2·63	3·13	3·00	3·41	2·88	3·56
	Sept.		3·36	3·54	4·00	3·78	3·70	4·64
	Oct.	*3·50	4·31	4·13	5·00	4·47	3·69	5·19
	Nov.		3·88	3·84	5·00	4·83	4·75	4·78
	Dec.	4·33	4·41	4·13	5·00	4·91	5·00	4·68
1882	Jan.	†3·63	4·22	4·19	5·00	4·97	3·50	4·53
	Feb.	5·53	5·13	4·75	5·75	3·94	3·13	3·98
	Mar.	3·75	3·24	3·23	3·80	3·03	3·25	3·18
	Apr.	2·47	2·50	2·72	3·00	3·28	2·31	3·41
	May	2·41	2·47	2·69	3·00	3·28	2·19	3·22
	Jun.	2·18	2·28	2·53	3·00	3·25	2·25	3·30
	Jul.	1·31	2·00	2·38	3·00	3·25	2·13	3·59
	Aug.	2·09	3·17	3·44	3·50	3·06	2·56	3·47
	Sept.	3·60	4·03	4·03	4·60	3·15	4·70	4·48
	Oct.	2·81	3·88	3·91	5·00	3·27	3·06	4·69
	Nov.	3·44	3·70	3·81	5·00	3·19	5·13	4·66
	Dec.	4·30	3·89	3·89	5·00	3·22	3·30	4·63

* One observation only.

† This has heretofore been variously stated as day-to-day money, short loans on Government securities etc., but from 1882 on is indicated as floating money rate.

Table 30 (continued)

		Day-to-day money	3 Months bank bills	6 Months bank bills	Bank rate	Paris market rate	New York call rate	Berlin market rate
Years	Months			(% figures)				
1883	Jan.	3·66	3·47	3·55	4·75	3·25	2·88	3·56
	Feb.	3·50	3·17	3·14	3·75	2·91	2·56	2·72
	Mar.	2·90	2·85	2·83	3·00	2·50	4·20	2·78
	Apr.	2·66	2·83	2·84	3·00	2·56	3·88	2·69
	May	3·09	3·52	3·64	3·75	2·53	2·31	2·66
	Jun.	3·43	3·48	3·64	4·00	2·64	1·90	3·15
	Jul.	3·25	3·61	3·70	4·00	2·66	1·81	3·13
	Aug.	3·25	3·63	3·96	4·00	2·58	1·95	2·95
	Sept.	2·25	2·61	2·94	3·50	2·53	1·81	3·22
	Oct.	1·66	2·58	2·78	3·00	2·64	2·13	3·47
	Nov.	1·45	2·24	2·75	3·00	2·63	2·10	3·35
	Dec.	2·53	2·67	2·94	3·00	2·66	2·13	3·41
1884	Jan.	1·72	2·36	2·72	3·00	2·69	1·75	2·94
	Feb.	2·72	3·24	3·44	3·38	2·72	1·56	2·34
	Mar.	3·00	2·75	2·86	3·13	2·28	1·63	2·59
	Apr.	1·69	1·81	2·16	2·50	2·41	1·56	2·91
	May	1·23	1·70	2·19	2·50	2·38	6·25	2·80
	Jun.	1·09	1·67	2·16	2·25	2·44	2·25	2·94
	Jul.	1·38	1·17	1·97	2·00	2·63	1·56	2·69
	Aug.	0·82	1·55	2·25	2·00	2·50	1·50	2·55
	Sept.	0·97	1·44	2·16	2·00	2·03	1·31	2·91
	Oct.	2·00	2·73	3·38	3·00	2·53	1·45	3·23
	Nov.	3·81	4·08	3·75	5·00	2·66	1·25	3·41
	Dec.	4·31	4·19	3·52	5·00	2·59	1·19	3·69
1885	Jan.	3·30	3·76	3·58	4·80	2·75	1·00	3·33
	Feb.	3·69	3·53	3·25	4·00	2·72	1·00	2·50
	Mar.	3·28	3·28	3·06	3·75	2·78	0·88	3·09
	Apr.	1·69	2·64	2·78	3·50	2·75	1·00	3·88
	May	0·65	1·51	1·94	2·70	2·38	1·00	3·05
	Jun.	0·47	0·83	1·28	2·00	2·25	1·00	2·78
	Jul.	0·43	0·79	1·46	2·00	2·58	1·00	2·63
	Aug.	0·50	1·31	2·14	2·00	2·16	1·00	2·31
	Sept.	0·44	1·59	2·59	2·00	1·84	1·00	2·75
	Oct.	0·50	1·30	2·23	2·00	2·30	1·60	2·73
	Nov.	1·22	2·27	2·63	2·75	2·47	2·00	2·72
	Dec.	2·59	2·86	2·91	3·50	2·41	2·00	3·09
1886	Jan.	1·63	2·29	2·59	3·60	2·58	1·60	2·28
	Feb.	0·88	1·45	1·86	2·50	2·47	1·63	1·66
	Mar.	1·16	1·63	1·94	2·00	2·28	1·88	1·88
	Apr.	1·25	1·76	2·08	2·00	2·60	1·70	1·83
	May	1·63	2·03	2·14	3·00	1·78	1·75	1·72
	Jun.	0·81	1·20	1·48	2·63	1·09	1·50	2·00
	Jul.	0·85	1·08	1·58	2·50	2·25	2·50	1·73
	Aug.	1·34	2·13	2·55	2·75	2·25	2·75	1·78
	Sept.	1·50	2·38	2·77	3·50	1·81	4·50	1·84
	Oct.	2·15	2·85	3·00	3·70	2·30	5·60	2·58
	Nov.	2·38	3·14	3·17	4·00	2·47	4·25	2·66
	Dec.	3·43	3·72	3·40	4·60	2·55	4·40	3·85

9

Table 30 (continued)

		(% figures)					
Years Months	Day-to-day money	3 Months bank bills	6 Months bank bills	Bank rate	Paris market rate	New York call rate	Berlin market rate
1887 Jan.	2·59	3·28	3·19	5·00	2·78	3·00	3·25
Feb.	3·03	2·98	2·89	4·00	2·59	3·13	3·06
Mar.	2·31	2·45	2·41	3·50	2·09	3·38	2·38
Apr.	1·05	1·21	1·45	2·60	2·33	4·50	2·00
May	0·59	1·00	1·41	2·00	2·16	4·25	2·03
Jun.	0·56	1·06	1·45	2·00	2·16	5·75	2·28
Jul.	0·63	1·39	2·08	2·00	2·55	4·60	1·88
Aug.	1·09	2·45	2·91	3·00	2·34	3·88	1·69
Sept.	3·08	3·65	3·63	4·00	2·08	4·40	2·30
Oct.	2·59	3·28	3·28	4·00	2·53	3·50	2·28
Nov.	2·38	3·06	3·03	4·00	2·69	3·38	2·28
Dec.	2·15	2·86	2·86	4·00	2·73	3·30	2·48
1888 Jan.	1·28	1·84	2·03	3·38	2·72	2·88	1·75
Feb.	1·25	1·56	1·97	2·75	2·34	1·75	1·47
Mar.	1·90	1·49	1·65	2·20	2·03	2·90	1·83
Apr.	1·25	1·47	1·69	2·00	2·25	2·13	1·56
May	1·59	2·08	2·25	2·75	2·25	1·50	1·59
Jun.	1·10	1·24	1·58	2·60	2·15	1·20	1·73
Jul.	0·84	1·30	2·06	2·50	2·38	1·00	1·47
Aug.	1·43	2·65	2·93	2·90	2·15	1·40	1·68
Sept.	2·91	3·48	3·58	3·75	2·78	2·00	2·47
Oct.	3·31	3·60	3·72	5·00	3·88	1·88	3·31
Nov.	2·65	3·46	3·45	5·00	3·85	1·90	3·08
Dec.	4·81	4·17	3·84	5·00	4·03	3·88	3·63
1889 Jan.	1·94	2·72	2·84	4·13	3·53	2·38	2·34
Feb.	2·31	2·55	2·53	3·00	2·50	1·75	1·56
Mar.	2·53	2·74	2·68	3·00	2·43	2·10	2·19
Apr.	2·06	1·69	2·00	2·75	2·31	2·38	1·50
May	1·15	1·56	1·93	2·50	2·20	2·20	1·58
Jun.	1·22	1·42	1·91	2·50	2·47	2·50	2·25
Jul.	1·19	1·42	2·41	2·50	2·53	2·69	1·78
Aug.	2·08	2·86	3·30	3·10	2·23	2·40	2·15
Sept.	3·34	3·78	3·81	4·25	2·38	3·75	3·16
Oct.	3·16	3·75	3·75	5·00	2·47	5·50	4·09
Nov.	3·28	4·04	3·96	5·00	2·88	3·40	4·73
Dec.	3·00	3·77	3·67	5·00	2·88	6·25	4·81
1890 Jan.	5·40	4·48	4·20	6·00	2·66	8·40	3·93
Feb.	5·41	4·38	4·10	5·50	2·44	2·88	3·53
Mar.	3·41	2·91	2·97	4·13	2·31	3·00	3·81
Apr.	1·75	1·95	2·28	3·38	2·44	4·00	2·94
May	1·38	1·83	2·38	3·00	2·58	4·80	2·93
Jun.	2·91	2·91	3·19	3·25	2·66	3·63	3·75
Jul.	3·81	3·88	4·09	4·00	2·66	3·25	3·16
Aug.	3·90	3·95	4·05	4·60	2·50	4·20	3·13
Sept.	3·51	3·94	4·03	4·25	2·53	3·63	3·56
Oct.	4·25	4·90	4·55	5·00	2·90	3·30	4·68
Nov.	4·94	5·69	5·69	6·00	2·97	3·75	5·22
Dec.	2·50	4·06	4·13	5·00	2·84	2·50	5·09

Table 30 (continued)

Years	Months	Day-to-day money	3 Months bank bills	6 Months bank bills	Bank rate	Paris market rate	New York call rate	Berlin market rate
				(% figures)				
1891	Jan.	1·68	2·33	2·63	3·90	2·18	2·70	3·40
	Feb.	2·75	2·50	2·66	3·00	2·47	2·50	2·59
	Mar.	2·19	2·44	2·63	3·00	2·84	2·88	2·69
	Apr.	2·19	2·75	2·94	3·25	2·88	2·75	2·72
	May	3·45	4·05	4·11	4·50	2·80	3·75	2·88
	Jun.	1·38	2·30	2·77	3·50	2·22	2·50	3·22
	Jul.	0·53	1·56	2·35	2·50	2·60	1·65	3·33
	Aug.	0·47	1·69	2·75	2·50	2·41	2·06	3·28
	Sept.	0·59	2·30	3·16	2·63	2·25	3·69	3·28
	Oct.	1·35	2·91	3·36	3·20	2·70	2·91	3·20
	Nov.	2·53	3·17	3·14	4·00	2·53	3·75	3·22
	Dec.	1·59	2·22	2·38	3·63	2·34	2·38	2·97
1892	Jan.	1·20	1·88	2·33	3·30	2·70	2·05	1·93
	Feb.	2·31	2·30	2·47	3·00	2·28	1·56	1·56
	Mar.	1·75	1·81	2·06	3·00	1·53	1·75	1·47
	Apr.	1·18	1·20	1·63	2·50	1·85	1·85	1·55
	May	0·50	0·98	1·44	2·00	1·22	1·69	1·34
	Jun.	0·50	0·88	1·34	2·00	1·13	1·56	1·75
	Jul.	0·53	0·88	1·53	2·00	1·93	1·65	1·45
	Aug.	0·50	1·02	2·00	2·00	1·31	1·75	1·44
	Sept.	0·80	1·08	2·18	2·00	1·14	3·45	1·75
	Oct.	0·78	1·77	2·47	2·50	2·03	4·50	2·22
	Nov.	1·53	2·50	2·78	3·00	2·28	4·63	2·38
	Dec.	1·40	1·90	2·20	3·00	2·20	4·80	2·85
1893	Jan.	0·75	1·34	1·81	2·88	2·28	3·00	1·72
	Feb.	1·09	1·59	1·84	2·50	1·97	2·63	1·28
	Mar.	1·98	1·58	1·83	2·50	2·03	2·85	1·80
	Apr.	1·44	1·63	1·88	2·50	2·28	3·69	2·09
	May	2·91	3·70	3·70	3·63	2·13	3·13	2·91
	Jun.	1·75	1·75	2·15	2·90	2·15	5·80	2·73
	Jul.	0·97	1·53	2·44	2·50	2·34	4·31	3·09
	Aug.	2·38	3·86	3·80	4·00	2·22	2·88	4·13
	Sept.	2·43	2·60	2·86	4·20	2·15	2·60	4·58
	Oct.	0·72	1·83	2·41	3·00	2·34	2·19	4·56
	Nov.	1·19	2·34	2·86	3·00	2·34	1·63	4·50
	Dec.	2·53	2·48	2·75	3·00	2·43	1·25	4·40
1894	Jan.	1·03	1·67	2·13	3·00	2·34	1·00	2·72
	Feb.	1·88	1·91	2·13	2·38	2·34	0·94	1·72
	Mar.	1·68	1·30	1·50	2·00	2·03	1·10	1·90
	Apr.	1·22	1·31	1·39	2·00	1·97	1·00	1·50
	May	0·94	1·08	1·39	2·00	1·34	1·00	1·78
	Jun.	0·63	0·72	1·06	2·00	1·69	1·00	1·75
	Jul.	0·38	0·65	1·01	2·00	1·72	1·00	1·44
	Aug.	0·30	0·60	1·02	2·00	1·30	1·00	1·48
	Sept.	0·28	0·56	0·86	2·00	1·30	1·00	1·91
	Oct.	0·41	0·56	0·97	2·00	1·80	1·00	1·63
	Nov.	0·48	0·83	1·18	2·00	1·94	0·95	1·50
	Dec.	0·63	0·88	1·19	2·00	1·63	1·19	1·66

Table 30 (continued)

Years	Months	Day-to-day money	3 Months bank bills	6 Months bank bills	Bank rate	Paris market rate	New York call rate	Berlin market rate
			(% figures)					
1895	Jan.	0·28	0·63	0·83	2·00	1·81	1·19	1·44
	Feb.	0·66	1·12	1·30	2·00	1·88	1·50	1·41
	Mar.	1·10	1·17	1·14	2·00	1·45	1·90	1·58
	Apr.	0·78	0·80	0·98	2·00	1·69	1·94	1·50
	May	0·40	0·80	0·95	2·00	1·63	1·45	1·73
	Jun.	0·44	0·59	0·81	2·00	1·53	1·25	2·03
	Jul.	0·28	0·59	0·77	2·00	2·13	1·19	1·63
	Aug.	0·45	0·64	0·79	2·00	0·98	1·00	1·55
	Sept.	0·38	0·64	0·81	2·00	1·31	1·50	2·50
	Oct.	0·38	0·63	0·82	2·00	1·78	2·13	2·56
	Nov.	0·70	1·17	1·24	2·00	1·80	2·05	2·93
	Dec.	0·70	0·98	1·03	2·00	1·78	3·06	3·34
1896	Jan.	0·45	1·06	1·21	2·00	1·73	3·70	2·93
	Feb.	0·63	1·03	1·11	2·00	1·66	3·25	2·31
	Mar.	0·56	0·74	0·88	2·00	1·66	2·81	2·06
	Apr.	0·41	0·62	0·76	2·00	1·78	3·13	2·16
	May	0·80	0·90	0·90	2·00	1·80	2·20	2·65
	Jun.	0·56	0·74	0·77	2·00	1·75	2·19	2·78
	Jul.	0·43	0·64	0·73	2·00	1·75	1·85	2·40
	Aug.	0·53	0·93	1·03	2·00	1·47	3·50	2·50
	Sept.	0·88	1·75	1·92	2·50	1·75	3·44	3·41
	Oct.	2·23	2·65	2·70	3·40	1·86	5·05	4·10
	Nov.	3·47	3·65	3·19	4·00	1·88	3·31	4·56
	Dec.	3·25	3·34	3·00	4·00	1·84	1·75	4·72
1897	Jan.	2·00	2·69	2·71	3·80	1·95	1·75	3·38
	Feb.	1·50	1·88	1·88	3·00	1·83	1·72	2·63
	Mar.	1·53	1·55	1·56	3·00	1·75	1·78	2·94
	Apr.	0·83	1·25	1·36	2·60	1·80	1·50	2·50
	May	0·59	0·95	1·20	2·13	1·84	1·50	2·34
	Jun.	0·66	0·95	1·27	2·00	1·78	1·16	2·59
	Jul.	0·45	0·85	1·31	2·00	1·83	1·23	2·43
	Aug.	0·63	1·49	2·03	2·00	1·78	1·25	2·66
	Sept.	0·91	2·02	2·53	2·13	1·81	1·56	3·25
	Oct.	1·43	2·46	2·61	2·80	1·95	2·63	3·90
	Nov.	2·34	2·90	2·78	3·00	1·97	1·75	4·16
	Dec.	2·78	2·94	2·76	3·00	2·00	2·10	4·18
1898	Jan.	1·59	2·45	2·47	3·00	2·00	2·19	3·16
	Feb.	2·69	2·69	2·56	3·00	1·83	1·78	2·59
	Mar.	2·69	2·95	2·87	3·00	1·78	1·56	2·72
	Apr.	2·48	3·60	3·60	3·80	1·93	2·20	3·13
	May	2·69	3·27	3·20	3·88	1·78	1·84	3·28
	Jun.	0·91	1·46	1·94	3·00	1·75	1·31	3·59
	Jul.	0·50	1·21	1·94	2·50	1·80	1·13	3·30
	Aug.	0·38	1·41	2·36	2·50	1·78	1·56	3·22
	Sept.	1·23	2·16	2·63	2·70	1·78	3·00	3·65
	Oct.	2·91	3·47	3·38	3·75	2·25	2·03	4·09
	Nov.	2·81	3·47	3·19	4·00	2·91	2·06	4·81
	Dec.	3·23	3·34	3·01	4·00	3·00	2·20	5·20

Table 30 (continued)

Years	Months	Day-to-day money	3 Months bank bills	6 Months bank bills	Bank rate	Paris market rate	New York call rate	Berlin market rate
				(% figures)				
1899	Jan.	1·38	2·34	2·47	3·75	2·95	2·59	4·38
	Feb.	1·75	2·08	2·19	3·00	2·83	2·38	3·63
	Mar.	2·55	2·38	2·34	3·00	2·80	3·65	4·28
	Apr.	1·81	2·23	2·27	3·00	2·83	3·19	3·69
	May	1·53	2·23	2·31	3·00	2·89	3·06	3·59
	Jun.	1·83	2·18	2·33	3·00	2·80	2·90	3·90
	Jul.	2·53	3·44	3·42	3·38	2·81	3·31	4·00
	Aug.	2·31	3·56	3·72	3·50	2·78	3·00	4·44
	Sept.	2·10	3·58	3·79	3·50	2·80	3·78	4·83
	Oct.	2·91	4·64	4·64	5·00	3·00	3·63	5·09
	Nov.	3·00	4·63	4·56	5·00	3·00	4·25	5·59
	Dec.	4·90	6·13	5·85	6·00	3·30	3·95	5·98
1900	Jan.	2·19	3·79	3·88	4·88	4·06	3·25	4·53
	Feb.	2·83	3·71	3·78	4·00	3·41	2·16	4·09
	Mar.	3·80	3·88	3·88	4·00	3·43	3·15	5·18
	Apr.	3·50	4·03	4·02	4·00	3·50	2·81	4·41
	May	2·72	3·53	3·61	3·88	3·25	1·88	4·50
	Jun.	1·85	2·61	2·93	3·20	2·80	1·63	4·80
	Jul.	2·41	3·34	3·84	3·50	2·89	1·47	4·03
	Aug.	3·30	3·88	4·11	4·00	2·76	1·33	4·05
	Sept.	3·38	3·83	4·05	4·00	2·72	1·53	4·44
	Oct.	1·78	3·89	4·13	4·00	3·00	3·06	4·03
	Nov.	3·20	3·97	4·06	4·00	2·93	3·80	4·18
	Dec.	3·31	4·02	4·05	4·00	3·00	4·19	4·56
1901	Jan.	3·03	4·16	4·25	5·00	2·94	2·75	3·59
	Feb.	3·88	3·85	3·87	4·50	2·55	1·75	3·16
	Mar.	3·78	3·71	3·70	4·00	2·75	2·20	3·73
	Apr.	3·31	3·56	3·56	4·00	2·73	3·31	3·44
	May	3·13	3·68	3·68	4·00	2·63	14·75	3·18
	Jun.	2·06	2·97	3·06	3·13	2·06	3·06	3·16
	Jul.	1·94	2·59	3·11	3·00	2·00	3·06	2·84
	Aug.	1·43	2·36	3·07	3·00	1·90	2·18	2·28
	Sept.	1·56	2·40	2·88	3·00	1·69	3·81	2·69
	Oct.	1·81	2·44	3·05	3·00	2·34	2·81	2·81
	Nov.	2·98	3·39	3·44	4·00	2·72	3·40	3·66
	Dec.	3·56	3·46	3·45	4·00	2·78	4·81	3·08
1902	Jan.	2·35	3·03	3·08	3·80	2·80	4·43	2·25
	Feb.	2·75	2·75	2·75	3·00	2·47	2·25	1·84
	Mar.	2·88	2·95	2·68	3·00	2·23	3·75	1·84
	Apr.	2·78	2·76	2·76	3·00	2·22	3·75	1·75
	May	2·60	2·79	2·80	3·00	1·88	4·65	2·03
	Jun.	2·56	2·63	2·66	3·00	2·17	2·69	2·28
	Jul.	2·22	2·49	2·67	3·00	2·41	2·63	1·63
	Aug.	2·53	2·70	3·01	3·00	1·99	3·35	1·73
	Sept.	2·41	2·97	3·33	3·00	1·97	6·44	2·41
	Oct.	2·45	3·43	3·49	4·00	2·53	7·30	2·75
	Nov.	2·84	3·55	3·48	4·00	2·97	4·53	3·13
	Dec.	3·75	3·90	3·80	4·00	2·81	5·75	3·41

Table 30 (continued)

		Day-to-day money	3 Months bank bills	6 Months bank bills	Bank rate	Paris market rate	New York call rate	Berlin market rate
Years	Months			(% figures)				
1903	Jan.	2·95	3·43	3·43	4·00	2·86	4·45	2·50
	Feb.	3·69	3·42	3·36	4·00	2·80	2·81	1·91
	Mar.	3·72	3·66	3·50	4·00	2·91	4·75	2·69
	Apr.	3·50	3·47	3·45	4·00	2·89	4·75	2·50
	May	3·13	3·46	3·46	3·80	2·71	2·35	3·03
	Jun.	2·59	2·85	2·93	3·25	2·56	2·31	3·28
	Jul.	1·90	2·42	2·91	3·00	2·68	2·75	2·95
	Aug.	1·78	2·82	3·16	3·00	2·30	1·88	3·28
	Sept.	3·00	3·80	3·95	4·00	2·63	2·06	3·69
	Oct.	2·58	3·68	3·81	4·00	2·73	2·30	3·38
	Nov.	3·28	4·00	3·95	4·00	2·84	3·38	3·47
	Dec.	3·28	3·69	3·70	4·00	2·86	4·56	3·56
1904	Jan.	2·85	3·25	3·29	4·00	2·83	3·00	2·70
	Feb.	2·94	3·38	3·28	4·00	2·56	1·69	2·78
	Mar.	2·63	2·99	3·05	4·00	2·69	1·81	3·44
	Apr.	2·78	2·56	2·66	3·50	2·71	1·45	2·93
	May	1·31	2·05	2·27	3·00	2·36	1·56	3·09
	Jun.	2·03	2·09	2·22	3·00	1·72	1·28	2·91
	Jul.	2·48	2·46	2·75	3·00	1·43	1·00	2·68
	Aug.	2·38	2·88	3·16	3·00	1·20	0·88	2·59
	Sept.	1·70	2·53	2·96	3·00	1·35	1·43	2·93
	Oct.	1·81	2·59	2·80	3·00	2·28	1·88	3·66
	Nov.	2·59	2·96	3·17	3·00	2·58	2·50	4·06
	Dec.	2·43	2·84	2·84	3·00	2·49	3·05	3·88
1905	Jan.	2·19	2·51	2·63	3·00	2·55	2·16	2·53
	Feb.	2·94	2·47	2·38	3·00	2·09	2·25	1·94
	Mar.	2·53	2·24	2·13	2·60	1·74	2·85	2·18
	Apr.	1·75	2·07	2·18	2·50	1·97	2·94	1·84
	May	2·28	2·20	2·34	2·50	1·59	2·44	2·28
	Jun.	1·75	1·88	2·08	2·50	1·74	2·53	2·28
	Jul.	1·34	1·73	2·16	2·50	1·84	2·25	2·09
	Aug.	1·31	1·95	2·24	2·50	1·34	1·94	2·19
	Sept.	1·73	2·78	3·01	3·10	1·75	2·70	2·98
	Oct.	3·25	3·98	3·95	4·00	2·72	4·88	3·94
	Nov.	3·13	3·97	3·83	4·00	3·06	5·69	4·41
	Dec.	2·65	3·54	3·48	4·00	3·03	8·00	4·88
1906	Jan.	3·25	3·70	3·40	4·00	2·69	4·38	3·91
	Feb.	4·06	3·86	3·41	4·00	2·45	4·50	3·31
	Mar.	3·78	3·45	3·07	4·00	2·78	4·55	4·08
	Apr.	2·81	3·20	3·18	3·50	2·94	12·13	3·34
	May	3·16	3·68	3·59	4·00	2·50	3·25	3·41
	Jun.	2·50	3·35	3·34	3·80	2·53	2·80	3·65
	Jul.	1·84	3·11	3·38	3·50	2·63	2·19	3·47
	Aug.	2·33	3·22	3·48	3·50	2·25	3·80	3·43
	Sept.	3·30	4·03	4·15	3·88	2·67	4·25	4·31
	Oct.	3·66	5·13	4·81	5·25	2·91	4·13	4·75
	Nov.	5·08	5·88	5·08	6·00	2·95	4·55	5·23
	Dec.	4·84	5·78	4·89	6·00	3·00	12·25	5·59

Table 30 (continued)

Years	Months	Day-to-day money	3 Months bank bills	6 Months bank bills	Bank rate	Paris market rate	New York call rate	Berlin market rate
				(% figures)				
1907	Jan.	4·00	4·85	4·42	5·50	3·00	2·63	5·03
	Feb.	4·56	4·74	4·28	5·00	3·00	2·81	4·59
	Mar.	3·93	4·96	4·78	5·00	3·15	3·85	5·40
	Apr.	2·44	3·66	3·92	4·50	3·31	2·25	4·56
	May	2·70	3·23	3·30	4·00	3·35	2·35	4·45
	Jun.	3·69	3·79	3·91	4·00	3·36	3·25	4·69
	Jul.	2·47	3·53	4·03	4·00	3·31	3·63	4·44
	Aug.	2·83	4·20	4·71	4·30	3·31	2·45	4·50
	Sept.	2·84	3·91	4·34	4·50	3·41	2·38	5·06
	Oct.	3·22	4·27	4·47	4·50	3·34	8·13	4·84
	Nov.	5·10	6·45	5·88	6·70	3·83	5·40	6·55
	Dec.	5·28	5·91	5·00	7·00	3·84	6·50	7·13
1908	Jan.	4·05	4·19	3·96	5·00	3·33	3·30	4·95
	Feb.	3·72	3·61	3·31	4·00	2·53	1·88	4·50
	Mar.	3·25	2·81	2·75	3·25	2·47	1·94	4·50
	Apr.	2·38	2·56	2·69	3·00	2·69	1·63	4·06
	May	1·80	2·12	2·58	2·90	2·18	1·85	3·90
	Jun.	1·31	1·34	1·89	2·50	1·66	1·56	3·28
	Jul.	0·98	1·27	2·38	2·50	1·40	1·25	2·78
	Aug.	0·88	1·50	2·40	2·50	1·09	1·16	2·81
	Sept.	0·97	1·40	2·31	2·50	1·66	1·44	3·16
	Oct.	1·18	1·91	2·35	2·50	1·98	1·50	2·85
	Nov.	1·69	2·23	2·41	2·50	2·13	1·81	2·47
	Dec.	2·32	2·25	2·28	2·50	2·31	2·69	2·97
1909	Jan.	2·20	2·49	2·51	2·80	2·48	2·10	2·30
	Feb.	2·25	2·25	2·15	3·00	1·23	2·06	2·19
	Mar.	2·94	2·12	1·97	3·00	1·25	1·88	2·69
	Apr.	1·28	1·38	1·52	2·50	1·38	1·85	2·05
	May	1·13	1·40	1·67	2·50	1·13	1·88	2·41
	Jun.	1·59	1·77	2·20	2·50	1·41	1·63	2·94
	Jul.	1·00	1·39	2·15	2·50	1·30	1·83	2·30
	Aug.	0·93	1·46	2·31	2·50	1·25	2·31	2·13
	Sept.	0·81	1·53	2·25	2·50	1·56	2·56	2·97
	Oct.	2·80	3·48	3·49	3·90	2·38	3·75	3·88
	Nov.	4·53	4·23	4·03	5·00	2·78	4·25	4·47
	Dec.	4·35	3·76	3·36	4·60	2·75	4·63	4·23
1910	Jan.	2·38	2·94	2·91	3·75	2·63	3·13	3·03
	Feb.	1·72	2·30	2·36	3·13	2·50	2·66	2·91
	Mar.	2·53	3·16	3·22	3·50	2·22	2·75	3·55
	Apr.	3·68	3·80	3·60	4·00	2·40	3·60	3·18
	May	3·28	3·48	3·33	4·00	2·19	3·44	3·25
	Jun.	3·13	2·65	2·77	3·13	2·19	2·73	3·31
	Jul.	1·53	2·06	2·64	3·00	2·08	2·30	3·10
	Aug.	1·88	2·67	3·48	3·00	2·00	1·34	3·38
	Sept.	1·95	3·09	3·49	3·20	2·28	1·85	3·88
	Oct.	3·16	4·08	3·93	4·50	2·91	2·88	4·22
	Nov.	5·00	4·42	3·97	5·00	2·81	2·81	4·58
	Dec.	3·58	3·57	3·38	4·50	2·53	3·20	4·55

Table 30 (continued)

Years	Months	Day-to-day money	3 Months bank bills	6 Months bank bills	Bank rate	Paris market rate	New York call rate	Berlin market rate
				(% figures)				
1911	Jan.	3·53	3·70	3·50	4·38	2·56	2·84	3·59
	Feb.	2·91	3·12	2·92	3·75	2·31	2·38	3·09
	Mar.	3·20	2·35	2·25	3·10	2·33	2·28	3·33
	Apr.	2·66	2·42	2·49	3·00	2·23	2·27	2·91
	May	1·69	2·20	2·40	3·00	2·16	2·38	2·81
	Jun.	1·83	2·19	2·76	3·00	2·13	2·28	3·33
	Jul.	1·31	2·03	2·88	3·00	2·19	2·38	2·41
	Aug.	1·44	2·65	3·48	3·00	2·16	2·34	3·00
	Sept.	1·85	3·34	3·68	3·40	3·08	2·30	4·10
	Oct.	2·22	3·75	3·75	4·00	3·50	2·30	4·34
	Nov.	2·44	3·45	3·33	4·00	3·38	2·34	4·50
	Dec.	3·58	3·79	3·46	4·00	3·30	4·10	4·65
1912	Jan.	3·47	3·63	3·34	4·00	3·34	2·41	3·34
	Feb.	3·56	3·37	2·93	3·63	3·09	2·14	3·78
	Mar.	3·28	3·44	3·16	3·50	3·18	2·48	4·70
	Apr.	3·13	3·40	3·33	3·50	3·19	2·81	3·75
	May	2·58	2·93	3·12	3·10	3·00	2·64	3·98
	Jun.	2·63	2·86	3·34	3·00	2·88	2·59	4·19
	Jul.	2·41	2·96	3·63	3·00	2·56	2·91	3·38
	Aug.	2·30	3·21	3·78	3·20	2·63	2·65	3·95
	Sept.	2·31	3·66	3·88	4·00	2·88	5·00	4·44
	Oct.	2·88	4·41	4·34	4·50	3·13	5·16	4·13
	Nov.	3·83	4·82	4·56	5·00	3·73	4·90	5·20
	Dec.	4·34	4·85	4·38	5·00	3·88	5·81	5·97
1913	Jan.	4·12	4·64	4·23	5·00	4·00	3·35	4·73
	Feb.	4·84	4·78	4·31	5·00	3·92	3·16	5·19
	Mar.	4·53	4·78	4·30	5·00	3·97	4·31	5·88
	Apr.	3·34	3·89	3·81	4·75	4·00	3·31	4·59
	May	3·15	3·71	3·75	4·50	3·95	2·99	5·25
	Jun.	3·69	4·25	4·56	4·50	3·75	2·19	5·47
	Jul.	3·00	4·13	4·72	4·50	3·75	2·19	4·63
	Aug.	3·03	3·83	4·29	4·50	3·60	2·30	4·73
	Sept.	2·84	3·83	4·25	4·50	3·75	2·81	5·38
	Oct.	4·00	4·84	4·76	5·00	3·80	3·68	4·70
	Nov.	4·56	4·91	4·66	5·00	3·75	3·72	4·34
	Dec.	4·53	4·81	4·47	5·00	3·56	4·50	4·47
1914	Jan.	2·60	3·28	3·14	4·20	3·53	2·98	3·25
	Feb.	1·56	2·14	2·22	3·00	2·94	1·81	3·03
	Mar.	2·53	2·15	2·14	3·00	2·75	1·84	3·34

SOURCE: *The Economist*. The day-to-day money rate was variously given in *The Economist* as the rate for 'day-to-day money', 'short loans on government securities to the Stock Exchange' etc. and from 1882 onwards was indicated as the rate for 'floating money'. *The Economist* did not always record the rates for three months' bank bills. Sometimes the rates were for 'two and three months' bills' and sometimes simply for 'short bills'. Evidently such digressions would cause only minimal errors in the calculation of the average rates for three months' bank bills. In these cases, too, the rates are treated as those for three months' bank bills.

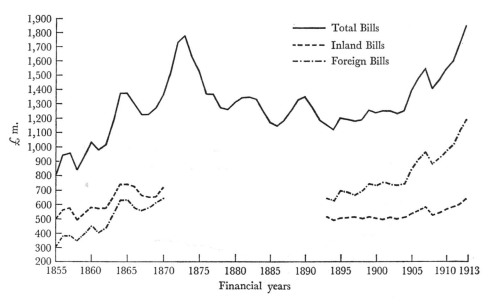

Fig. 1. *Amounts of bills drawn, 1855–1913*

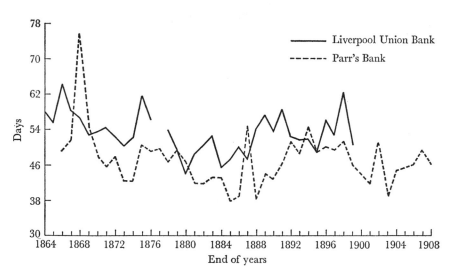

Fig. 2. *Unlapsed currency of bills held by Parr's Bank
and Liverpool Union Bank*

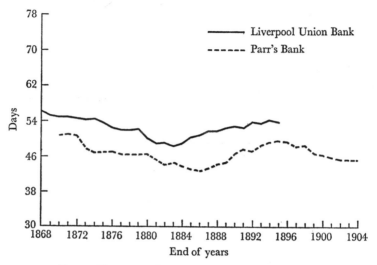

Fig. 3. *Nine-year moving average of unlapsed currency of bills held by Parr's Bank and Liverpool Union Bank*

BIBLIOGRAPHY

OFFICIAL DOCUMENTS

Commissioners of Inland Revenue, 1856–69, *Report*, BPP 1870, Vol. 20.

Commissioners for Her (His) Majesty's Inland Revenue, *Reports*, BPP 1883 and later years.

Select Committee on the High Price of Bullion, 1810, *Minutes of Evidence*, BPP 1810, Vol. 3.

Select Committee on the State of Commercial Credit, 1811, *Report*, BPP 1810–11, Vol. 2.

Secret Committee on the Expediency of the Bank Resuming Cash Payments, 1819, *Minutes of Evidence*, BPP 1819, Vol. 3.

Select Committee on the Law relating to Merchants, Agents, or Factors, 1823, *Minutes of Evidence*, BPP 1823, Vol. 4.

Select Committee on Promissory Notes in Scotland and Ireland, 1826, *Minutes of Evidence*, BPP 1826, Vol. 3.

Select Committee on Manufactures, Commerce and Shipping, 1833, *Minutes of Evidence*, BPP 1833, Vol. 6.

Secret Committee on Joint Stock Banks, 1837, *Report*, BPP 1837, Vol. 14.

Select Committee of the House of Lords appointed to inquire into the Causes of the Distress among the Commercial Classes, and how far it has been affected by the Laws for Regulating the Issue of Bank Notes payable on Demand, 1847, *Minutes of Evidence*, BPP 1857, Session 1, Vol. 2.

Secret Committee on Commercial Distress, 1847–48, *Minutes of Evidence*, BPP 1847–8, Vol. 8.

Select Committee on Bank Acts, 1857, *Minutes of Evidence*, BPP 1857, Session 2, Vol. 10.

Select Committee on the Operation of Bank Acts, 1857–58, *Minutes of Evidence*, BPP 1857–8, Vol. 5.

Select Committee on Banks of Issue, 1875, *Minutes of Evidence*, BPP 1875, Vol. 9.

Royal Commission on Depression of Trade and Industry, 1886, *Minutes of Evidence*, BPP 1886, Vol. 21.

Royal Commission appointed to inquire into the Recent Changes in the Relative Values of Precious Metals, 1887, *First Report: Minutes of Evidence*, BPP 1887, Vol. 22.

Committee on Finance and Industry, 1931, *Minutes of Evidence*.

(United States) National Monetary Commission, *Interview on the Banking and Currency Systems: Interview with Sir Felix Shuster*, 1910.

Miscellaneous Statistics for the U.K.

BOOKS

Ashton, T. S., 'The Bill of Exchange and Private Banks in Lancashire, 1790–1830' in *Papers in English Monetary History*, ed. by T. S. Ashton and R. S. Sayers, Oxford, 1954.

Bagehot, W. *Lombard Street*, London, 8th ed., 1882.

Balogh, T. *Studies in Financial Organisation*, Cambridge, 1950.

Bloomfield, A. I. *Short-Term Capital Movement under the Pre-1914 Gold Standard*, Princeton, 1963.

Fry, Henry. *The History of North Atlantic Steam Navigation*, London 1896.

Gregory, T. E. *The Westminster Bank through a Century*, London, 1936.

Hawtrey, R. G. *A Century of Bank Rate*, London, 2nd ed., 1962.

Homer, S. *A History of Interest Rates*, New Brunswick, New Jersey, 1963.

King, W. T. C. *History of the London Discount Market*, London, 1936.

Leatham, W. (*First Series*) *Letters on the Currency addressed to Charles Wood*, London, 1840.
(*Second Series*) *Letters to William Rayner Wood*, London, 1841.

Macardy, J. *Outline of Banks, Banking and Currency on the Basis of Manchester*, Manchester, 1842.

Mitchell, B. R. and Deane, P. *Abstract of British Historical Statistics*, Cambridge, 1962.

Morgan, E. V. *The Theory and Practice of Central Banking 1797–1913*, Cambridge, 1943.

Paish, F. W. *Long-Term and Short-Term Interest Rates in the United Kingdom*, Manchester, 1966.

Palgrave, R. H. I. *Notes on Banking in Great Britain and Ireland, Sweden, Denmark and Hamburg: with some remarks on the amount of bills in circulation, both inland and foreign, in Great Britain and Ireland; and the Banking Law of Sweden*, London, 1873.

Peake, E. G. *An Academic Study of Some Money Market and Other Statistics*, London, 1923.

Pressnell, L. S. 'The Rate of Interest in the Eighteenth Century' in *Studies in the Industrial Revolution*, ed. by L. S. Pressnell, London, 1960.

Sayers, R. S. *Gilletts in the London Money Market, 1867–1967*, Oxford, 1968.

Scammell, W. M. *The London Discount Market*, London, 1968.

Sykes, J. *The Amalgamation Movement in English Banking, 1825–1924*, London, 1926.

Tooke, T. and Newmarch, W. *A History of Prices*, London, 1857.

PERIODICAL ARTICLES

Barnett, R. W. 'The Effect of the Development of Banking Facilities upon the Circulation of the Country', *Journal of the Institute of Bankers*, 1881.

Davis, L. E. and Hughes, J. R. T. 'A Dollar-Sterling Exchange, 1803–1895', *Economic History Review*, 2nd Series, 1960.

Dick, James, 'Banking Statistics—A Record of Nine Years' Progress', *Journal of the Institute of Bankers*, 1884.

'Banks and Banking in the United Kingdom in 1891', *Journal of the Institute of Bankers*, 1892.

'Banking Statistics of the United Kingdom in 1896 compared with former years', *Journal of the Institute of Bankers*, 1897.

Dun, John. 'The Banking Institutions, Bullion Reserves and Non-Legal-Tender Note Circulation of the United Kingdom', *Journal of the Royal Statistical Society*, 1876.

Jackson, F. H. 'The Draft on London and the Tariff Reform', *Economic Journal*, 1904.

Knauerhase, R. 'The Compound Steam Engine and Productivity Changes in the German Merchant Fleet, 1871–1887', *Journal of Economic History*, 1968.

Neisser, H. 'Der internationale Geldmarkt vor und nach dem Kriege', *Weltwirtschaftliches Archiv*, $xxix_2$, 1929.

Newmarch, W. 'An Attempt to Ascertain the Magnitude and Fluctuation of the Amount of Bills of Exchange (Inland and Foreign) in Circulation at one time in Great Britain', *Journal of the Statistical Society*, 1851.

Williams, T. T. 'The Rate of Discount and the Price of Consols', *Journal of the Royal Statistical Society*, 1912.

PRINCIPAL PERIODICALS

Bankers' Magazine.

Banking Almanac.

Economic Journal.

Economic History Review.

The Economist.

Journal of Economic History.

Journal of the Institute of Bankers.

Journal of the (Royal) Statistical Society.

The Statist.

INDEX

DATE D